Homeschooling
for
College Credit

Jennifer Cook – DeRosa

FOR ALL THE AMAZING PARENTS

ACKNOWLEDGEMENTS

With enthusiasm to Sgloer, my bridge to things possible. Thanks for setting up Instantcert, the best testing resource on the web.

A special acknowledgement to my favorite classmates and IC family:

4dkids, a4tunatemom, Alissaroot, Alleycat, Barcotta, Basket Weaver, Blu2blu, Bmills072200, BrandeX, Bricabrac, Burbuja0512, Cframe, Chebasaz, CLEP101, Creationstory, dc67, Dcan, Farmerboy, Gary, Gcalvin, Geezer, Gus, HawkGuy, HorseManiac, Irnbru, Jadechow, jec959, Jonathan Whatley, kiwi lover, LatinTea, Levi, Librevore, Lindagrr, Maniac Craniac. Mapalo, Marianne202, MISin08, Mlwilliamsiv, MomOfMany, NAP,NJ593, Okiemom, OldRustyPipe, OnMyWay, Operalady, P00057870, PatsGirl1, Peace123, ponyGirl93, rebel100, Rickyjo, Rmroberts, Ruddigore, Ryoder, SandraNC, Scholar Interrupted, Shadowless, ShawnA, ShotoJuku, Shunshine, sirJake, snazzlefrag, Soupbone, STG, Studyhard, Sunshine, Tasman, Thatbrian, TMW2010, Yenisei, **and the many new classmates I've met this year.**

CONTENTS

YOU'RE A HOMESCHOOL GUIDANCE COUNSELOR!

Chapter 1 Resource Summary:

Accelerated Distance Learning, Brad Voeller.
Global Publishing, 2001

What Color is Your Parachute, Richard N. Bolles.
Ten Speed Press, 2011

Occupational Outlook Handbook, US Department
of Labor Bureau of Labor Statistics. 2012.
http://www.bls.gov/oco/

Home School Legal Defense Association
www.hslda.org

Robinson Curriculum
www.robinsoncurriculum.com

What about High School?

When we first told our family and friends that we were going to home school our son Matt for preschool in 1994, homeschooling wasn't as common as it is now. I didn't receive a lot of support, and I didn't fully grasp the extent of what home schooling would mean for our family.

I think most people assumed we would send our children to school, eventually. School registrations came and went, and little by little, we became a full-fledged home school family. As I grew comfortable as "the teacher" and my children began to read, I knew we could do this for years to come. When I was asked how long we planned to homeschool, I always answered "as long as it works," which is still how I answer.

When my oldest son started 8th grade, I began to panic. In one short year, he would start high school! Multiple friends and family members noticed this too, and many suggested that high school would be the perfect time to transition out of home school. Ironically, the academics were the least of my fear. Academics are what many homeschool families worry about, but by now, I knew where to find curriculum and support. Instead, I felt unequipped to be his high school guidance counselor! What about transcripts? What about college prep? Oh-no! I didn't even know what a **transcript** was. I felt completely out of my depth, and we were at a fork in the road.

Deciding to Jump In

When you make the decision to move forward through high school, new issues present themselves. Issues like creating a transcript, documenting credit, figuring out a GPA, standardized tests, college prep courses, career decisions, and finally, what about the prom? (Just kidding). High school, for me, was the scariest aspect of homeschooling. I felt that for the first time, someone else would get to evaluate my ability to run our home's school, someone very important. "College Admissions" would decide my child's future based on whether or not I did a good job for the past 17 years. The worst part, for me, was there would be no re-do if I messed up. I was ready to bail-out when I read a very interesting book.

A homeschool graduate, Brad Voeller, detailed his journey toward earning a bachelor's degree in his book *Accelerated Distance Learning (2001)*. While I didn't have experience with distance learning, or anything accelerated, I became encouraged. At least one person had walked this path successfully, and he put his suggestions in print. At the time, traditional homeschool books rarely addressed the transition from high school to college, and traditional college books hardly addressed homeschooling.

Mr. Voeller's book was a "light-bulb moment" for me. In *Accelerated Distance Learning*, Mr. Voeller explained how he tested out of many college courses at home, and earned legitimate credits toward his degree;

before he was 18! He reinforced to me what I already knew. There is always more than one way to get what you want, don't let anyone tell you differently. Putting Mr. Voeller's suggestions to the test, I earned a semester's worth of college credit in-between diaper changes and swimming lessons. If I could do it, I knew I could teach my children to do it too.

The landscape of education has changed drastically in the past decade. Education is more accessible than ever. Homeschooling is more common, community support exists for homeschooling families, and we have HSLDA in Washington protecting our freedom. Now, more than ever, we have digital information, connected by an internet, which allows us unprecedented access to information.

Bias, propaganda, and agenda

As you start to research homeschooling, high school, and college, you'll notice nearly every helpful source has some form of bias. Why is this? Because, people are human. It's natural to recommend your alma mater, or your state's school, or the school that Billy's neighbor's sister's friend was accepted to. We take lay advice with a grain of salt. What we generally don't expect, is that our college admissions counselor has a bias. A college admissions counselor is an employee, their job description is to advise you and your child on your options at *that college*. It's like asking Pepsi what they think of Coca-Cola, likely, not much.

Friends, who work in career and technical fields, tend to suggest degrees aimed at job training. Degrees "in" something tangible make the most sense. (Nursing, business, accounting, landscape, etc.) In contrast, adults working in social science or humanities suggest a path that allows you to follow your passion. (Art, music, writing, psychology, etc.) Neither is right, but you should always recognize the bias that colors every suggestion.

You'll also hear strong opinions about 2 year and 4 year options degrees, for-profit vs non-profit schools, and several other forms of criteria. There is nothing wrong with a suggestion or indulging the pros and cons of various options. Your launching point for this process must start with the premise that *every college is a business*, and *every business has an agenda*. College publications are propaganda, and everyone working in academia has a bias. Once you accept that premise, you can begin the real research. Your responsibility is to sort through the facts and opinions. Once you grasp the key facts and opinions about higher education, you'll be the best high school guidance counselor your child could have ever hoped for!

Throughout this book, you'll receive a sprinkling of my biased advice too. After all, I'm human, and have opinions about some of the great (and not so great) traditions of college preparation. Having over 18 years of experience as a community college educator, I've seen the strengths and weaknesses of the community college system, and I'll share those with you. I've also logged **thousands of hours** breaking down the facts and opinions of this process, and I'll share them with you in homeschool-speak.

My personal belief is that you should try to get through your undergraduate education (associate or bachelor's degrees) with zero to no debt, so my suggestions are heavily colored by the cost of each option. To maintain the highest integrity, I will always call an opinion and opinion, and a fact a fact. In other words, I hope to be a source you will trust. It is also my belief that getting into college is no great accomplishment, but getting out of college (with a degree) is very difficult, and should be the goal. Your decisions will determine how many barriers you create or remove for your child.

Your job description

As your child's high school guidance counselor, you will take on one of the most exciting aspects of your child's homeschool experience. Through your diligence, you'll collect facts, weigh opinions, and develop a plan of attack. You'll conduct the "behind the scenes" research, and collect enough information to facilitate all of your children into the college of their choosing.

You will begin to appreciate CLEP, ACE, and accreditation the way some people appreciate fine wine. Armed with this book, you'll begin to assemble a 4 year plan for your high school student that will yield him a fantastic amount of college credit to use as he pleases.

As with any job, your own level of motivation and attention to planning will determine the level at which you implement my strategies; and as with any child, their ability and motivation will intersect with your plan at a level unique to him.

Guiding your child

Guiding your child toward a career is not as easy as it sounds. Each family has their own perspective on money-vs-happiness, following your heart vs providing for your family. In addition, perhaps moral or religious practices will dictate some decisions. Does gender or career choice matter?

Let's be frank. If you believe, in your heart, that your daughter's primary adult responsibility is to be a wife and mother, possibly a homeschool mother, then getting her ready for med school is a bad plan. After she invests 12 years in her education (and student loan debt to exceed $270,000) she isn't going to be able to simply put that on hold to raise a family. Logically, she'll feel compelled to do the work she has trained for. Financially, she is morally obligated to repay her debt, and brings a great burden into the family if she cannot do so. These issues should be addressed early, not later. Later, things are more complicated. Consider also, that encouraging your child to earn a degree in an obscure field with little job opportunity takes her down a path of college debt and future of job insecurity. For a young person starting a family, this makes life difficult.

There are no right and wrong paths, but exploring how a career choice maps ones future is important. Conversations about gender roles, sacrifice of different professions, and financial rewards can begin in childhood. If religion is part of your family's belief system, this should not be left out of the career planning discussions. You have earned the privilege of being your child's career counselor; this is not the time to push family values out the window. This is not a path to walk alone. Speak up!

Guiding your child: middle school

Starting as early as middle school, you can begin conversations with your child about their future aspirations. Many excellent resources exist to help you guide your child. Don't use this time to zero in on a career, rather begin helping your child find their purpose. Having a purpose and using a talent are two very enjoyable activities. For example, if your child has a strong entrepreneurial spirit, encourage him to follow through. By starting a small business like lawn mowing, he gets to feel the accomplishment that comes from working for one's self. While he likely won't go on to own his own lawn company, the act of starting a business and working for oneself allows the entrepreneurial spirit to grow. The confidence to be a self-starter will overflow into any path he later chooses.

One excellent resource is the book *What Color is Your Parachute?* By Richard Bolles. This book isn't for the 12 or 13 year old, this book is for you! Mr. Bolles does an excellent job teaching you to assess your aptitude as well as ability. By learning, how he pulls these into tight focus, you will help your child do the same. You probably have a good idea of their strengths and weaknesses by now, and you can discuss these with your child. As you already know, strengths and weaknesses don't guarantee anything, but it's a good place to start as you help your child ponder their future.

The middle school years are an excellent time to lay the groundwork for deliberate consideration. In other words, many children mow lawns or baby sit, and many parents know their child's strengths; you will use these situations to deliberately help your child consider how these activities help them become an adult, and perhaps choose their career.

Academically, the middle school years are when many children fall apart. Lacking a solid foundation in math or reading will spell disaster for your high school student. As the subject matter will get more complicated, you must use the middle school years to fill any gaps. This might mean going backwards in math, or even changing your curriculum approach, but remember that 100% understanding of arithmetic is more useful than a vague understanding of algebra and geometry.

Many states have curriculum requirements, but you still have the responsibility for your child's education. You must give your child the best education within your power. If you need to address deficiencies in your child's foundation, double check that you'll be in compliance with your state laws. A quick visit to Home School Legal Defense Association website can provide you with your state's legal summary and requirements. If you live in a state that allows it, you may want to drop everything except for reading and math for 1 semester. An intense focus for 1 semester could not only correct any deficiency, but send you child over their grade level.

For any child, a curriculum centered on the "3 R's" is never a bad idea. One such curriculum is The Robinson Curriculum. If your child is entering high school unable to read good literature, it's worth your consideration to look into this approach. The creator of the approach, Dr. Robinson, used nothing but the 3 R's to educate his children. His children, all now grown adults who hold doctorate degrees, fared very well academically.

Guiding your child: high school

Early in high school, the first year or two, you should help your child explore career options. Don't be surprised to learn that your child likely has no idea what a particular job is, how much it pays, or what it means. I remember giving a lecture at the community college. I addressed a group of prospective culinary students. One girl in the front row was barely listening, until I began to talk about money. I explained that everyone in the room wanted to become chefs, but to remember that most restaurants only had one chef and most of you will spend the majority of your careers as cooks vying desperately for a promotion. I explained that a chef's salary was fine, but the years leading up to that required living on a cook's wage. A minimum wage, or at best a couple dollars above it. This student nearly jumped out of her seat! She let out a "whoop!!!" so loud that everyone laughed. I was confused, and asked her what she was so excited about? She responded that she had been earning minimum wage for the past year, and the thought of getting a dollar an hour more was fantastic news! I tried to explain that a dollar an hour over minimum wage feels like a lot of money when you're 18, but it would be hard to raise a family on that wage. The point of the lecture was how to separate yourself and rise to the position of Chef; so you can one day support a family. I'm afraid she missed my point, caught up in the extra money she'd make this year.

A child doesn't understand the difference between careers requiring 40 hours per week, or ones requiring working "on call." A child doesn't value the importance of having health insurance, vacation time, or holidays off. These quality of life issues are very real, and something you should talk about. Fortunately, our children have had their father home for birthdays, holidays, and weekends.

For most chefs, this is never the case.

One aspect I'm very direct about with my children is salary. Is salary everything? No, of course not. But let's remember that a child has no real concept of salary. Eventually, you'll want your child to be able to support him and your grandchildren! The fact is, when your child gets a job for minimum wage, he will feel like a millionaire! I use a measure that my children easily understand, and even my 11 year old grasps. I use what they know- our lifestyle. We own a home, two cars, and take an occasional vacation. I also shop thrift stores, grow my own vegetables, and clip coupons. They hear the word "no" often.

When one of my children ask about a job, I'll say "that job pays half of your dad's pay check" or "that job pays 10 of your dad's pay checks." That phrase removes the necessity for them to understand dollar figures and just lets them ponder what that would mean in terms of lifestyle. These discussions are about "things" but teens understand "things" very easily.

If your child's prospective career will require him to live below your family's current standard of living, this is a valuable point that shouldn't be overlooked. As your child's guidance counselor, you should counsel.

As your child moves through high school, you can begin aligning them with opportunities to meet real people in careers. Consider this a "live" career fair. Start with friends, neighbors, family, church members, homeschool colleagues, and other adults in your community. People who know your child are likely to accept a meeting eagerly. By sending your child to meet individuals in their place of work (dressed appropriately, of course) he will experience a wide variety of situations that he may find interesting- or may end up hating! Knowing what you *don't* want to do with your life is also valuable!

If possible, help your child arrange "job shadows" in professional settings. In a job shadow, you "shadow" someone through their day. Sometimes, you can do small tasks and other times you may only observe. While some work or legal regulations may dictate the parameters of his job shadow, he can likely get a great taste of the career. I once did a job shadow 2 days per week for 4 weeks in a nurse practitioner's office. I logged about 40 hours of observation time, and some real work experience. This helped me decide whether or not I wanted to pursue a career in nursing, and in my case, I didn't. This was a valuable lesson, and ultimately, my job shadows in the kitchen grabbed my heart.

The best print resource, hands down, for unbiased job information is the United States Department of Labor. The Department of Labor's Bureau of Statistics publishes a guide every year called The Occupational Outlook Handbook. The handbook is on their website, and very easy for the public to use. (Free!) In the handbook, every job in every industry is reported on. Trends in the field, future expectations for growth, education, training, working conditions, salary expectations, and industries that do the most hiring are all included for the current year. This is a "must see" for anyone exploring careers. I suggest this site for parents as well as their teen. Teach your teen how to navigate the online handbook, and require that they use it when doing their own exploration.

Sample high school plan- hypothetical

We will explore high school planning in detail later, but what will this look like for you and your child? This small hypothetical plan shows you how we will inject college-earning options into your child's high school years. We will take regular courses your child may take anyway (History, French, Math, and Government) and plan them in a way that allows their "final exam" to be a credit earning exam. Some simple planning might look like this table:

	High school course	Potential college credit
9th	Algebra 1 History 1 French 1* 9th Grade English	US History 1 CLEP, 3 cr.
10th	Algebra 2 History 2 French 2* 10th Grade English	Algebra CLEP, 3 cr. US History CLEP 2, 3 cr.
11th	Trigonometry American Govt. French 3 11th Grade English	Literature CLEP, 6 cr. Trigonometry CLEP, 3 cr. Government CLEP, 3 cr.
12th	Calculus 1 French 4* English 101	Calculus CLEP, 3 cr. French CLEP, 12 cr English 101, 3 cr.

*cumulative knowledge is necessary in French

The plan above, if executed exactly, yields 39 college credits. This is college credit for courses your child was probably going to take anyway. The difference is that we planned them to work alongside college exams and courses. 39 college credits translate into OVER ONE YEAR of college credit. If your child is of average intelligence and average to above average motivation, this plan is realistic and inexpensive.

For a child who plans to earn an Associate Degree after high school, he will graduate from homeschool with roughly ½ of the degree completed! For the Bachelor's Degree candidate, shaving 1 ½ years off of tuition also means shaving 1 1/2 years off of dormitory stays, and about 16 fewer text books. At over $100 each, removing text books from the equation will always save a great deal of money.

The hypothetical plan is also not aggressive. It is for an average student. For an aggressive student, you can complete dual-enrollment options at the local community college (taking a class for both high school and college credit) and even coordinate more exams into your plan through Advanced Placement courses and other brands of exam credit. I've observed motivated high school students **complete** their associate and bachelor degrees in high school! It can be done.

As we advance through the next several chapters, you'll learn about multiple credit earning options available to your high school student. My caution is that you don't become so invested in your child earning credit that you overlook the joys of homeschooling. At the end of the day, even a child that graduates with 1 college class (3 credits) has shaved 16 weeks of homework and about $1000 off the cost of his degree. That is an awesome accomplishment! As the parent, you'll be able to orchestrate your child's classes in a way that generates college credit. The exam credit isn't instead of the courses; it's in addition to them. There is nothing to lose. For the average student, this is absolutely possible. For the motivated student, allow him to read this book when you're finished. Working together on a goal is going to maximize your family's success to a much greater degree.

This is going to be awesome!

So if you take a moment to think about the potential time and money saved, you'll realize how exciting this journey will be. Beyond being the guidance counselor, you have the added benefit of being your child's number one cheerleader! Yes, it's going to require you to learn some new terminology, create a plan, and follow through over several years. It will also (likely) require revision from time to time. That's what this book will help you with. There is no reason to become anxious about this journey; I'll guide you in the right direction. Look at your hard work and planning as a "scholarship" that you can give to your child!

The exact path is to be determined by your child. Even your best planning will ultimately be at the mercy of his ambitions and ability. Whatever credit your child earns, even if it's just one, is a step in the right direction. So get ready, this is going to be awesome!

THE TOP 10 SOURCES OF COLLEGE CREDIT

FOR YOUR HIGH SCHOOL STUDENT

Chapter 2 Resource Summary:

The College Board www.collegeboard.org
Thomas Edison State College www.tesc.edu
DSST/DANTES www.getcollegecredit.com
Clovis Community College www.clovis.edu
New Mexico Junior College www.nmjc.edu
Rosetta Stone www.rosettastone.com
American Council on Teaching
American Council on Education
www.acenet.edu
ALEKS Math www.aleks.com
Straighterline Courses
www.straighterline.com
Harvard University www.harvard.edu
Excelsior College www.excelsior.edu
Black Hawk College www.bhc.edu

Let's hit the ground running. While many of these sources will be visited again in future chapters, I wanted to jump right in and get you thinking about all of the potential credit sources available to you and your child. By the time you are reading this book, there may even be new sources available!

The top 10 sources of college credit for your high school student:

1. CLEP

I discuss CLEP frequently in multiple chapters, mainly because it is my personal favorite credit source. I've taken (and passed) 15 CLEP exams. My exams translated into 60 college credits, most of which I used in my bachelor's degree. CLEP is the brand name of a test, published by The College Board.

CLEP exams are multiple choice tests graded as pass/fail. There are no high or low scores, no essays, and no letter grade. A numeric score is generated based on the number of questions you got correct. There is no penalty for wrong answers. The score is a scaled score, in other words, it is graded on a curve. A best-guess estimate for passing a CLEP exam is answering about 50% of the questions correct. The exact formula and scores remain tightly confidential. The reward for passing a subject exam is 3 college credits, and 6 college credits for the general exams. For those competent in a foreign language exam, a passing score awards 6 credits, while a high pass awards 12!

This exam an excellent fit for any homeschool student because there is no age requirement (simple parental waiver for children under age 13 on internet based exams). If you're 14 or 84, anyone can take any CLEP exam at any time. CLEP scores are saved for 20 years, so even if your child does not attend college in this decade, he has the next two decades to use the credit. At the time of this printing, a CLEP exam costs $80.00.

CLEP exams are available in each of the liberal arts (general education) as well as business. There are 33 exams, all available to your student. While it's unrealistic to take every exam, there are a possible 150 credits available to earn. Since an entire Associate's degree is only 60 credits, you can appreciate the usefulness of these exams.   A conservative estimate is that your college will accept at least 15 CLEP credits. In a college with a generous CLEP policy, expect 45 for more credits allowed toward a degree. The college I attended for my Bachelor's degree (Thomas Edison State College, NJ) has no limit on CLEP, as long as it meets the requirement for your degree. Approximately half of all colleges in the United States accept CLEP in some amount. Visit The College Board website to find a complete list.

A final word on CLEP; Lest you believe that the content is too far above your child's grade level, you would never take an exam "cold" and the study resources we will discuss later will do well to prepare even an average child for most of these exams. In addition, with more than half of all US colleges awarding CLEP credit, it's silly not to try. Failing the same exam 6 times is still cheaper than attempting the course ONE time at your state university.

What if your child fails? Good news, it's okay. Your scores are confidential, and only **you** decide if any school ever sees them. If you do fail, you simply wait the required 6 months and try again. You can repeat this process an unlimited amount of times. When you have passed all of the exams you want (at the end of 12th grade) you simply submit your official CLEP transcript (with passing grades only) to the college(s) of your choice.

CLEP exams can be attempted any business day during business hours, generally with only 24 hour notice required. Your score appears instantly as you end the exam. Every homeschooled child should be attempting multiple CLEP exams. Period

2. AP

AP (Advanced Placement) exams are also published by The College Board. The exam content is almost identical to CLEP, and many of the tests are the same, but these are different types of exams. An AP exam is offered only through your local high school. While this is not a problem, many high schools are happy to allow you test with their students, they are offered only once per year. This poses a problem for studying properly if you want to attempt multiple exams.

For some students, sitting in a group setting to take an exam is uncomfortable. CLEP exams, in contrast, are usually done in a private testing center with only one or two additional work stations. Adding in the potential red tape of testing at the high school, some may find these not worth the extra trouble.

There are a few similarities between both brands. First, cost is nearly identical, and scores are saved for 20 years. Why would your child use AP instead of CLEP? There are AP exams in some subjects for which AP is the only option. Latin, for instance is available through AP and not through CLEP. On the other hand, there are multiple brand options for exams; rarely is there ever only one brand option.

Sometimes, colleges don't accept CLEP but will accept AP. Those colleges tend to be highly selective. If your child is looking at only highly competitive top tier schools, you should consider using AP instead of CLEP. In addition, having good AP scores will strengthen his application. MOST APPLICANTS to highly competitive schools have many strong AP test scores; so in this case, AP is not used as a means of earning credit, rather to ensure competitiveness. This list would include the top 20 colleges in the country. If that's not where your child is headed, use CLEP instead.

The final significant difference between CLEP and AP is that AP includes free response questions. Most will require essays and fill-in-the blank answers. If writing, even for a math exam, isn't your strongest suit, it's possible to score poorly overall based on writing ability.
This test format requires a grader, so there is a delay receiving grades. Once graded, you'll receive a score 1-5. The lowest score is a 1, and the highest a 5. Many colleges award credit based on a minimum score (usually 3). For high scores, a 4 or 5, some colleges may award additional credit.   Some colleges use AP exams to place students ahead, or give them "advanced standing" instead of awarding credit. This, while flattering, does not save your child any time or money and is not necessarily a benefit to anyone except the college. In other words, it doesn't remove college requirements.

3. **DSST / DANTES**

The DSST / DANTES (names used interchangeably) exams used to be only available to our military; however they are open to the public and your children. A DSST exam is just like a CLEP. DSST is a lesser known brand, so it's possible that a simple web search at your college's website may not provide you with lists like you'll find for CLEP or AP. Rest assured that if your college accepts CLEP and AP, they likely accept DSST/DANTES as well. Be prepared to ask.

At the time of this writing, DSST exams cost $80 and also award 3 credits for most successful attempts. There are some exams offered through DSST that are not offered through CLEP or AP (eg. The Civil War). One point in DSST's favor, is that some of their exams have been determined to award "upper level" credit. Where CLEP and AP only award 100 and 200 level (freshman, sophomore) credit, DSST exams can earn 300 level (junior) credits. While this may not matter at the community college (100/200) level, this can be a benefit at the bachelor's degree level. Frequently if you can't find a CLEP testing center near you, you may be able to find a DSST testing center instead.

4. Community College Dual Enrollment

Hardly available 5 years ago, dual enrollment is hot now, and growing in popularity. You'll find dual enrollment information through your nearest community colleges. Community colleges have opened their doors to high school students, and it's an amazing opportunity. Dual enrollment is exciting, because the student is able to enroll prior to earning their high school diploma or GED, which was not previously the case. The student attends class, online or in person, along with the regular college class. Some states offer this for free; others charge full tuition, so you'll have to check your own community. Registration is always done through the college, not the high school. If you'd like, you can even search beyond your own state. Many community colleges are offering their distance learning courses as dual enrollment, so the location of the physical campus isn't relevant. With just over 2000 community colleges in the United States, this opens up a fantastic opportunity for homeschooled children.

As a homeschool family, your children have access to something a traditionally schooled child may not have. For instance, if your public high school already offers dual enrollment agreements with one local college, they will likely not allow your child to attend a college out of state to study another subject of interest, even if your child is up for the challenge. They limit and restrict enrollment, restrict eligibility requirements, and dictate their schedule. Homeschooled kids have no such restrictions. If you want to learn it, it's out there to learn!

In instances where tuition may be free (check with your local colleges) you'll still likely have to pay for text books. College text books are an unimaginable expense, one that we will address in a future chapter. Anticipate up to $200 per course text. If you're paying full price for dual enrollment, community college tuition averages $100 per credit, so a typical 3credit course will cost roughly $300 plus books and fees. At the time of this writing, the cheapest community college in the country is Clovis Community College in New Mexico, with New Mexico Junior College running a close second. Both participate in dual enrollment, and both offer distance course options. At around $50 per credit, you can't find a better tuition rate for graded courses. They hold regional accreditation, meaning the general education courses your child takes will transfer into nearly any university.

The down-side to dual enrollment is simple, if your child bombs the class, the grade on their permanent record. Many colleges require you to disclose all previously earned credit under penalty, so that "D" may forever be part of your child's GPA. For that reason, do not rush your child into a course before their ready, and consider taking only 1 course at first. Adjusting to a college schedule is difficult for most people of any age.

Lastly, in my own classroom as a college instructor, more than 90% of the "F" grades I've ever given have been due to a student who fails to withdrawal. They simply stopped attending, and didn't officially complete withdrawal paperwork. This is an automatic (and permanent) "F" on a transcript. In other words, never just *stop* attending class. If your child is not going to pass their class, for any reason, they need to report to student services and withdrawal. You may or may not get any of your tuition back, but you are protecting your GPA forever. Always withdrawal your child instead of allowing a failing grade for the course.

5. Foreign Language Exams

If you're starting early enough (9th or 10th grade) foreign language tests are a gold mine of credit. Unlike United States history or algebra, foreign languages take time and practice to master. So, while this won't be an option for all of my readers, it certainly applies to anyone starting early enough. In addition, even if English is not your first language, you are still eligible to take any of the foreign language exams for which you are functionally fluent. In fact, if you're already fluent, the credit is practically sitting there waiting for you to grab it.   For those starting from scratch, I have to recommend Rosetta Stone curriculum.
Regretfully, I did not discover Rosetta Stone until I already had 2 sons in high school, but we are taking full advantage with our younger children. My 10 old year works on French, and my 7 year old works German. If fluency follows, there will be more than enough time to test out, and maybe even learn a second language.

Rosetta Stone is expensive, however, you'll find good resale value, and you can try it for free on their website. Their approach to teaching is unique, and it is similar to the way a mother teaches her baby to talk. In other words, we don't learn reading and writing as an infant, we learn meaning first.

That is the brilliance of Rosetta Stone. You look at a picture and hear the word that means the picture. You learn understanding, not grammar. It's a very comfortable system, and user-friendly. For parents, you'll be able to log in and track your child's lessons as well. There isn't anything to "do" or "teach" in the program.

If you use Rosetta Stone, or some other foreign language program, you'll want to choose an exam that matches with your strengths. For instance, if you use CLEP, there is only listening and reading, no speaking. This might make the exam considerably easier for someone who finds speaking difficult. In our home, 1 level lasts 2 school years. Your mileage may vary. You can buy 1 level or all 5 levels if you're feeling ambitious, because it's a much better deal at around $500. 5 levels will easily take a full 4 years of high school, and maybe even 8th grade. What does a college charge to teach your child 2 years of language? $2,000-$5,000!

There are multiple testing options for those with moderate to excellent fluency. Awarding the most credit is the New York University Foreign Language Proficiency Exam. A difficult exam, you must demonstrate proficiency in reading, listening, and composing a 350-word essay. The cost is $200. This is exam is available in more than 50 languages, making it the top exam option available. The exam is a paper-pen test, and you use a local proctor to supervise your test. A passing score awards up to 16 college credits. This is the equivalent to two full years of college level language credit. Even if you have no intention of using the language in your career, that much credit can meet and exceed most of the general education humanities requirements in addition to some electives.

Second place easily goes to CLEP, which awards either 6 or 12 credits based on your score. A passing score yields 6 credits, while a high pass awards 12. At only $80 this exam is the best value. The exam consists of listening and reading only, but is only available for French, German, or Spanish. The test is taken on computer, and graded instantly. Fortunately, these are three very popular languages, and if you are looking to purchase a language curriculum secondhand you're more likely to find Spanish than Urdu. In the same breath, it'll be easier to resell "popular" language curriculum when you are finished with it.   Third place goes to Advanced Placement. AP exams are only offered once per year, and duplicate the subjects of CLEP (German, French, and Spanish) but also offer Chinese, Latin, Italian, and Japanese. AP exams test listening, reading, and writing, and award credit similarly to CLEP (6-12 credits, respectively). These exams are pen-paper based. With a written component, you'll have to wait patiently to find out your score. Priced under $100, these are still an excellent deal, but the additional written component, the added wait time, and the inconvenience of one test date per year place these at the bottom of my list in under user-friendliness.

Lastly, but worth mentioning is the America Council on Teaching Foreign Language Oral Exam. At the time of this writing, this oral-phone exam, is offered in more than 60 languages. These exams are ACE-evaluated for credit. Fewer colleges accept ACE-evaluated courses than I'd like to see, but if yours does, this might be a great option. These exams are conducted over the phone in the comfort of your own home or other location.

6. ACE-Evaluated Courses

ACE (American Council on Education) evaluates all types of courses, adult education, workplace development courses, and online learning experiences formally and makes recommendations for college credit. Not all colleges accept ACE evaluated courses, but that shouldn't stop you from considering them. I'll share a few of my favorite ACE sources of credit in a moment.

If your child has obtained an FAA pilot's license, they already have earned college credit. Initial pilot training is worth 5 credits, and they don't have to pay a dime, they already have it. You simply have to open an account with ACE (free) and provide documentation. Additional gems may include some CPR/first aid programs, management programs through McDonald's restaurant, Jiffy Lube employee e-training, oral foreign language proficiency (see Foreign Language in this chapter), Dale Carnegie courses, Microsoft certifications, SCUBA diving courses, and more. There are thousands of ACE-evaluated courses, and it's worth browsing the list. While it may not be cost or time-effective to seek out these *potential* sources of credit, for a child that's already in progress, it makes the best use of your time to grab them (for free) while you can.

My favorite source of ACE credit is ALEKS. ALEKS is an artificial intelligence math curriculum that's gaining popularity in the high school, community college, and homeschool community. In addition to it being a fantastic curriculum, they have so many math courses; you'll absolutely find one at your child's level. Not all of their courses are evaluated for college credit, so if you can't locate the specific list yourself, call ALEKS customer service. They are fantastic and you'll speak to a real person every time.

As I mentioned, ACE is not accepted by all colleges, but if you're going to learn math anyway, it's one of the few options you can do completely at home without proctored exams or visiting a college campus. ALEKS courses are excellent for middle school and up, but the lowest course for college credit is Intermediate Algebra. This is roughly the equivalent of Algebra 2. *I realize on the ALEKS website Beginning Algebra is lower than Intermediate Algebra and listed as available for college credit, however, this course is almost always identified as remedial; under 100 level learning.

ALEKS costs under $150 per year, and under their subscription plan you can take 1 course at a time, but upon passing the assessment exam with greater than 70%, you have "passed" the course and can have the course added to your ACE transcript. For those who are already loyal to a math curriculum, you can still cash in on ALEKS math credit. Simply continue with your child through pre-calculus and then upon completion of pre-calculus you can register your child with ALEKS. At that point, you'll pay 1 month's tuition ($20) and your child can start at Beginning Algebra, pass the assessment exam with 70% or better, and move up to the next course.

A child, who *already has math knowledge,* through another curriculum can complete ALEKS courses (assessment exams) in an hour, and walk away with potential credits. The entire course sequence (beginning algebra- trig/precal plus stats) can be completed easily inside of 1 month's tuition, because there is very little review necessary. If this is your plan, be sure to add each course to your ACE transcript before attempting the next since ALEKS does not maintain any records or transcripts of your child's progress.

My other favorite source of ACE evaluated courses is a company called Straighterline. Unlike ALEKS, Straighterline is not necessarily a great deal financially, however, there are aspects of these courses worth your attention. Straighterline courses are ACE evaluated, and they offer a good variety (where ALEKS only offers math). The monthly subscription is steep, $99, and you still pay per course ($40). In addition, you'll need a text book and lab pack for sciences. This can run you an additional $100-$300. If you catch a promotional rate, you can sometimes find a BOGO coupon or a 10-course bundle for $1000.

If it's not a guaranteed transfer, and it's expensive, why should you consider Straighterline? There are some learning style benefits that may suit your child better than a CLEP exam or attending a community college. Straighterline courses are self-contained and self-paced. The proctoring is done online with a web cam in your home. You also have some access to tutors and advisors that you don't have with ALEKS. Finally, Straighterline uses teachers to grade written work, and instant-grade exams for quizzes and tests.

Best practices for Straighterline are achieved when your child works quickly and independently. If your child can complete one (or two) entire courses in a month, you can reduce the overall cost considerably. I've known people who've complete entire 3-credit college courses through Straighterline in a weekend. If you're motivated, you can move through a course quickly and save time and money. If your child is average in motivation, or even below average, you can spend a lot of money for potential credit.

My son completed 2 courses in 1 semester, and despite using a discount code, it still cost about $600. If you're certain that your prospective college accepts ACE credit, the convenience of working at your own pace, in your own home, is really what sells this company. If you're unsure about potential credit, it's still a good self-contained system, with minimal to no parental involvement needed.

7. Prior Learning Assessments (PLA)

There's no question that many people have enjoyed earning credit through PLAs. Prior learning assessments can be a way to use eclectic experiences to your advantage, and earn college credit. PLA is different from ACE-Evaluated experiences, because in a PLA, you must prove your experiences to be credit-worthy, and submit them to your college for evaluation. Many colleges have PLA policy on their website, so you can usually find out if anyone in your area allows credit this way.

I'm not against PLAs in theory, however, in practice, they are highly impractical for a high school student. In addition, not all colleges allow "experience credit" (PLA). PLA credit really serves adult learners, especially those with extensive work experience. For example, a small business owner may be able to present a portfolio demonstrating they have already have competency in a course called Small Business Entrepreneurship. This enticement is for the new untapped adult market.

PLA generally involves creating a portfolio to demonstrate that you have mastered or achieved competence in an area that is the equivalent to a college level course. Having the experience is not what earns you credit, rather demonstrating ways that you have achieved competence is often required.

Let's assume your high school student has worked as a volunteer at the local zoo for several years. There may be aspects of that experience that could be used in a portfolio for college credit. Perhaps your child has spent time establishing a new exhibit, teaching classes, leading demonstrations, or hosting field trips. These experiences could be turned in to credit if they match a course competency, however, the experience itself is not the credit. Many colleges will discuss PLA portfolios with you, and perhaps send you an information packet if you're interested.   The down side of PLAs is that they don't always transfer, so if you anticipate that a transfer is inevitable, this might not be the best use of your time. Also, PLAs are not automatic. In other words, the credit can still be denied. Some portfolios are 50 pages or more, and that effort is wasted if you didn't demonstrate how the course competency was met.

Something else to consider, if your PLA is in a subject that is clearly not part of your regular degree, it's likely not a good idea. Why? Because the credit is going to be pushed down into an elective category, which in many cases, could have been accomplished in a fraction of the time for a fraction of the cost with a simple CLEP exam. Many schools use PLA as their carrot, to attract you to their program. While more often it is adults who are drawn to this option, be aware that PLA may not work best for everyone, and be sure to understand all of the requirements before enrolling. Also, before making a decision, evaluate other potential ways to earn the same credit, and proceed from there.

8. Summer School

Summer school is not to be confused with dual enrollment. Often, colleges have specific courses that they allow for dual enrollment, and a formalized application process. This is not generally the case with summer school. Many colleges, even Harvard University, allow high school students the opportunity to enroll for summer school. Sometimes this can include dorm experiences, sometimes you can use local colleges and simply commute, other schools take the students abroad, and others put courses online. Many times, summer is an "open enrollment" period, where students can enroll with little to no application red tape.

Like dual-enrollment, graded credits are forever, and a failed grade may have to be disclosed in future college applications. That said, summer school is a wonderful opportunity to earn 3 or more credits for future use. Most summer school programs range from 5-8 weeks, so they can be a faster pace than a traditional 16-week semester. For this reason, it may be best to limit your courses to 1 or 2. For overseas experience, you are generally limited to only that course. Speaking of Harvard University, visit their Continuing Education tab to see a full listing of their summer options for high school students. Every summer they have exciting and rigorous options for the motivated student, and they also have some of the most exciting study abroad experiences offered; and for what it's worth, it probably wouldn't hurt to see Harvard University on your child's future college applications.

9. ACE-Evaluated Exams

The top two players of ACE-evaluated exams are Thomas Edison State College of New Jersey which offers their Thomas Edison State College Exam Program (TECEP), and Excelsior College of New York which offers Excelsior College Exams (ECE). Both colleges are fully accredited colleges that offer equivalency exams for college credit. Like ACE-evaluated courses, the acceptance of credit wildly depends on the college. The structure of a TECEP or ECE exam is very similar to that of CLEP or DSST.

TECEP exams are about $100 and are text-book specific, meaning: you must use the suggested text for exam preparation. The exams are offered for 3 credits, and all levels (100-400) are available in a number of subjects. The exams are graded as pass/fail. TECEP exams are available over 20 subjects, and are taken pencil-paper style using a remote proctor that you secure. For my degree, I completed a TECEP exam, and found my local librarian happy to proctor my exam for me no charge.

ECE exams cover more than 50 topics, including nursing. ECEs are also text specific, but Excelsior does a great job of providing practice exams for their tests, though they are not free. Some practice exams cost upwards of $75. The exams vary from 2-6 credits, but the average cost is $275. ECEs are not graded as pass fail, they issue letter grades. There is some advantage to this, it can help a college accept the credit (some may have policies against pass/fail credit) and it can boost a GPA. On the other hand, like dual enrollment or summer school, a poor grade is part of your college transcript and stays with you forever.

For potential future nurses, ECEs make up the entire nursing degree program at Excelsior College. (The RN portion is completed locally) Excelsior College is the single largest nursing program in the United States and offers a nearly-distance learning option for associate degree RN nurses. Upon completion of general education courses and ECE nursing exams, students complete their clinical skills in a facility near their home before sitting the NCLEX (RN) exam.

10. Winter Break & Mini-semesters

A new trend among community colleges in which classes are crammed into a few weeks. Some schools, fortunately, have placed these courses online, making them accessible to anyone with a computer. Other schools require daily attendance, but just for a few days.

One of my favorite mini-mester schools is Black Hawk College (Illinois). They offer mini-mesters which take place entirely inside Christmas break. Most of these courses are 3 credits, and about half of the offerings are online. Having completed their Contemporary Sociology course this way, I didn't find the work load impossible. Their mini-mesters are exactly 14 days in length and cost about $100 per credit. For students enrolling in fewer than 6 credits, no placement or entrance tests are required. The application is free.

Harvard University (Massachusetts) offers my other favorite winter option, called "January session." Offered through the Continuing Education College, these on campus courses take place for 21 days in Cambridge. These courses are offered for undergraduate (associate or bachelor) or graduate credit (masters) and open to anyone. This credit will transfer into any college or university. There is no application fee, and no selection process. Simply enroll, and attend! Harvard doesn't provide dorm housing for January sessions, but will provide you names and numbers of potential sublet, rentals, hotels, and host families for your stay.

Check your local college's on-campus options, and any community college for distance learning options. In almost every instance, courses that are completed at a traditional college and courses at a traditional college via distance learning will not be distinguishable on a transcript. In other words, they do not indicate "online" on the student's transcript.

THINGS A COLLEGE REPRESENTATIVE WON'T TELL YOU

Chapter 3 Resource Summary:

United States Department of Education
Accreditation Database
http://ope.ed.gov/accreditation

American Military University & American
Public University (APUS) www.apus.edu

Dave Ramsey www.daveramsey.com

A college won't tell you things?

In the interest of good faith, let's assume that the college will answer any question you ask them directly. In this light, you have to know what to ask. In addition, departments can't answer questions for other departments, so unless you're asking the right person, your answer may be inaccurate. Finally, it doesn't matter what an advisor *told you*, or what you understood her to mean. The college catalog and other print material will always reign supreme. The college web site is a good place to start, but you need to find the written policy for anything important.

Understanding the college staffing and catalog rules will help you understand the potential barriers you can face when meeting with admissions or advisors personnel. In addition, unless you are enrolled, you are a *prospective* student. The college catalog and policy books apply to enrolled students only, not potential students. This requires you to be diligent about changes while your child is still in your homeschool.

Who are *advisors*? Advisors fall under the category of student services personnel. Student service personnel take care of everything besides instruction: admissions, financial aid, advising, registration, degree guidance, and graduation verification.

You'll interact with all of the student services personnel when you are a student, but as a *prospective student* you likely won't see an advisor. Most point of contact occurs with *an admissions representative*. All people who provide advice to you through this process are not "advisors" but you should always find out who they are and their role in your child's admissions. Sometimes, it's just a student (called "work study") covering phones!

So you don't accuse me of unwarranted paranoia, you can spend 15 minutes browsing the internet looking for admissions jobs. These job postings will request sales and marketing backgrounds. Many times, a degree is not even required. Why might a college want a salesman as the initial point of contact with your child? Because, admissions representatives are salesmen. Admissions representatives come from telemarketing, retail sales, and marketing companies. They are not teachers, they are not counselors. **Their job is to enroll your child at the school they currently work for.** If, next semester, they work for a competing college, they will similarly try and convince you to enroll down the street. It's what they are hired to do.

Lately, the for-profit colleges have been in the hot seat for using aggressive marketing and high pressure sales techniques, but let me tell you that non-profit colleges have the same agenda, they are just more careful. College is driven by enrollment ($), and the market is flooded with educational opportunities (and non-higher ed. opportunities like military service, apprenticeship, and trade school). The federal government will (literally) give any applicant a student loan, and the end result is an extremely high number of dollars available to colleges through enrollment.

There are more colleges than ever before, more trade schools, more online schools, and....more students. It is a buyer's market; your child will literally have their choice of where to attend college. That's not to say that there isn't competition to get into *certain colleges*, but more than half the accredited colleges are "open enrollment" schools, which means 100% of those qualified to apply are accepted. So, beyond looking at the top 2% of colleges, everyone in the remaining 98% is going to beg for your child. (...and the money he brings with him of course!) Keep that in mind as you research your options, besides a few exceptions, an accredited college degree is as good as any other accredited college degree.

You can (and should) do most of your planning through high school with the goal of removing barriers. Stop wondering if your child can get INTO college. He can. Your child needs to figure out how to GET OUT of college with a degree! 86% of high school graduates enter college, only 26% get out. Everyone, however, still repays their student loans.

Your research should help you remove potential barriers that prevent your child from gaining full access to credit they've earned in high school. We'll work on this more in coming chapters. By the end of this book, you won't need the college employees to help you plan your child's degree! In fact, you may not need them at all.

I'd like to share some of the points which I believe to be very important when making enrollment decisions. You have a choice where your dollar is spent, and sometimes the things that seem important to school choice, really are completely unimportant.

Accreditation
National Accreditation is less than Regional Accreditation.

Seem counterintuitive? Many schools are counting on you thinking so. Regional Accreditation is the gold standard for all colleges and universities who transfer credit back and forth. Each region of the United States has an accreditation body that dictates many of the rules and policies (though not all) that guide the college. Credit earned at a regionally accredited college (any region) will almost always transfer to another regionally accredited college (any region). All of your public state universities and community colleges are regionally accredited (RA), you can confirm this by looking on their website. This allows easy transferability among other RA colleges, and you can easily assume that any RA degree is equally legitimate as any other RA degree.

National accreditation is not so neat and tidy. There are numerous private parties that have formed their own accreditation process, and they have very official sounding names. Mix in with several of the outright illegitimate organizations and things can get very confusing very quickly. Nationally accredited (NA) colleges are not universally transferrable; in fact, most RA schools outright object to any credit transfer from NA colleges, and even disallow enrollment.

If your child obtains an associate's degree through an NA college, he is likely going to have a difficult time getting accepted in to an RA bachelor's program. Likewise, if you hold a NA bachelor's degree, getting into an RA masters or doctorate degree program is very slim.

Is this always true? No, there are exceptions, too many for me to explore in this book. What isn't open to an exception is the requirement of certain professionally licensed or certified positions. For instance, if you want to become a Certified Public Accountant, a K-12 teacher, a doctor, a nurse, a therapist, a veterinarian, and any number of other licensed professionals, a NA degree is strictly forbidden. If you have not yet enrolled your child in a class, simply investigate before doing so. You can check the US Department of Education database for the accreditation status of any approved school in the country. If you choose a NA school for your child's high school courses, do so with fully informed consent. Many of the NA schools are completely legal, and happen to be trade-specific (cosmetology, culinary arts) and completely appropriate. Just be aware ahead of time at the limits of the degree. Additionally, many trade-specific programs are also offered through RA community colleges, and usually for a fraction of the cost.

One potential deception technique, is a career school, trade school, etc. that also offers high school diplomas/certificates. These schools may hold Regional Accreditation for their high school programs (a completely different thing) and advertise so loudly on their websites, that you might wrongly assume that their college programs are also Regionally Accredited. Double check.

What if you have already started a high school or college class that is NA, and now you want to change to an RA school? You can contact your new potential college and see if your credits transfer. In my opinion, at the high school level, I would suggest simply completing the course and not reenrolling for the next semester. In high school, you still have flexibility and can explore a more appropriate college option later.

I found out about RA/NA the hard way. My first undergraduate degree, from THE top program in the country, wasn't regionally accredited at the time I attended. I would never have known, because my industry didn't care, had I not decided to return to college. I found that no one would give me credit for any of my course work. I was denied by 11 schools, including some big-box for profits that really wanted my money, but they wouldn't give me a single credit for my degree. This is an example of how a degree can have high industry utility, but may not have high academic utility. If you want to change paths and turn your NA credit into RA credit, you can use the American Public University or American Military University (both belong to a University system called APUS) that holds both national AND regional accreditation. Currently, they are the only university system in the United States that holds both. Since they hold both, they will accept transfer credit from either RA or NA, and when you graduate, you will hold an RA degree. I like to call this "laundering credit" because you essentially input NA credit and an RA degree is awarded. It's a beautiful option, and it's very reasonably priced. Despite the name, you do not need to be associated with the military to enroll, and they have very interesting degree options. Dual enrollment is on a case by case basis.

Regional Accreditation Bodies
1.   Middle States Association of Colleges and Schools
2.   New England Association of Schools and Colleges
3.   North Central Association of Colleges and Schools
4.   Northwest Commission on Colleges and Universities
5.   Western Association of Schools and Colleges
6.   Southern Association of Colleges and Schools

Developmental / Remedial Courses
Developmental classes can kill your degree plan.

Developmental classes are classes that number under level 100 (freshman). Most of the time you are never told the devastating impact of these courses, or why you have to take them. One thing's for sure, they will eat your money, your time, and turn your 2 year associate degree into a 3-4 year associate degree before you even enroll. With the burn out/drop-out rate exceeding 50%, you don't want to add barriers in front of your child's finish line.   Developmental classes are classes intended to "prepare" your child for the 100 level courses they need for their degree. As a rule, courses under level 100 never count toward your degree. You do, of course, still pay full price for them. Developmental courses typically are in math, reading, or writing. While your homeschooled child is undoubtedly bright, being caught on a bad day could inadvertently place him in a developmental class. Once you have been assigned a developmental track, you cannot jump ahead. In addition, you usually can't go back and test out after the fact.   How does this happen? Most colleges have a system in place that places your child into a level. In a 4-year university with competitive admission, ACT or SAT scores are used to predict readiness and placement tests are not necessarily used. Community colleges and open enrollment colleges are another story. These colleges accept any student at any academic level. Because of the wide range of readiness, colleges use placement tests like the ASSET or COMPASS. (Or an already scored ACT or SAT exam)

Often, and wrongly, admissions reps will simply instruct your child to wander down to the testing center at his convenience to take this exam. NO! Do not take these exams cold. These exams are the placement tests that determine whether or not you'll land in a developmental track or straight into your degree program.

The best line of defense is to avoid taking the test if possible. Many colleges will simply waive the exam if you have met minimum scores on the ACT or SAT exams. Others will waive the exam if you have X amount of transfer credit. CLEP exams would be included in this amount, so if your child has already passed 1 or more exams, ask for a waiver.

If your child must take the exam, study! Your child can use ACT or SAT type prep materials, as well as exam-specific study guides. Your college will tell you the specific brand of placement test being given, and you can locate practice tests for him to use online. If your child isn't testing high enough, you should consider waiting a semester before taking the test. In addition to it indicating a potential difficulty with college-level learning, you avoid the cost and time of completing developmental courses.

Here is a sample scenario of how a developmental course can derail a degree plan. The sample student is completing his "first two years" at his local community college before enrolling at his state university. He hopes to earn an Associate of Science degree as he progresses. The student plans to major in engineering, and must complete calculus-based physics before matriculating (transferring) to the university.

In order to take calculus based physics, the community college requires the student to be enrolled in, or finished with, calculus 2.

The sequence generally takes 4 semesters.

3 credits Calculus 1 MATH198
3 credits Calculus 2 MATH199
4 credits Physics 1 w/Lab PHYS101
4 credits Physics 2 w/ Lab PHY102

Your home school 12th grade student is currently finishing up algebra 2/geometry and getting ready for summer vacation. He has not completed Pre-Calculus (Trig), but hopes to take that course this summer at the community college and be ready for Calculus 1 by the start of the year.   You and your child meet with someone at the college and they are eager to get you signed up for summer session and help you map out a degree plan.

(English, History, etc., have been omitted to keep your attention on the math remediation)

(SUMMER: MATH175 Pre-Calculus)

YEAR 1
Semester 1 (FALL) MATH198 Calculus 1
Semester 2 (SPRING) MATH199 Calculus 2

YEAR 2
Semester 3 (FALL) PHY101 Physics 1 w/Lab
Semester 4 (SPRING) PHY102 Physic 2 w/Lab

The student services person informs you that your son must take a placement exam as soon as possible to register in time for summer. Since your son is completing Algebra 2, and the information on the exam only covers Algebra 1 and below, you decide to have your son take the exam tomorrow. Unfortunately, the student's placement test didn't go well because his on-screen calculator didn't work properly, and he had to rush through the last 6 questions, mostly guessing. Your son reported having several questions on statistics and probability, something he'd never studied. These problems were compounded by a noisy testing center.

The sample student tested into Beginning Algebra (Algebra 1) which is just a slight bit lower than they had hoped. Upon receiving his score report, the advisor calls in the family to introduce his new degree plan.

The new plan is as follows:

YEAR 1
SUMMER: MATH098 Beginning Algebra
Semester 1 MATH101 Intermediate Algebra
Semester 2 MATH121 College algebra w/Trig

YEAR 2
SUMMER: MATH126 Pre-Calculus
Semester 1 MATH198 Calculus 1
Semester 2 MATH199 Calculus 2

YEAR 3
Semester 3 PHYS101 Physics 1 with Lab
Semester 4 PHY102 Physics 2 with lab

As you can see, missing a few extra questions on his placement exam added 4 additional courses (indicated in **bold italics**) in front of his degree requirement, which started with Calculus 1. By the time the student has completed his Associate transfer degree, some of his peers may be graduating with their bachelor's degree. His bachelor's degree, if everything else goes perfectly, will take 5 ½ years of full time study.

Since this student must use financial aid, the school requires that he take 6 credits per semester minimum, so in addition to the math courses that won't count toward his degree, he'll also have additional general education courses that he'll take simply as fillers to meet his financial aid requirements. This student will likely complete 30 additional credits beyond what is necessary for his degree, and if his endurance allows, he will have spent no less than an additional $5,000-$10,000.

While the numbers in this scenario may be different at your college, the layers are not. You can ask for all of the layers of developmental courses for reading, writing (or English), and math. This will give you a better picture of what's in front of English 101 (likely 2-3 layers) and Math 101 (likely 1-3 layers). Developmental courses should be avoided if at all possible.

Transferring
Not all Associate degrees are equal.

Colleges, especially community colleges offer associate degrees. These are the typical 2-year degree that can either lead to direct employment or as a transfer into a 4-year college. Your community college likely offers: AA (Associate of Arts), AS (Associate of

Science), AAS (Associate of Applied Science), and AOS (Associate of Occupational Studies). The AA and AS are in one group, and the AAS and AOS are in the second group. The only thing these two groups have in common is their tuition rate. Buyer beware!

Let's look at AA and AS degrees. These are the degrees, that when you look at a college's website, seem somewhat boring. With titles like General Education or Liberal Arts, these don't sound nearly as enticing as degrees "in" something. AA and AS degrees (which are essentially the same thing depending on the college you attend, but both fill the same purpose) are designed to *transfer* into a 4-year program. These degrees have sometimes already been approved for transfer to other in-state colleges. The purpose of the degree is to complete all 60 general education credits. Courses like English, psychology, and math make up the degree plan. These are not preparing you for a career; they are preparing your mind for upper level college work. Provided you are working with a good degree planning advisor, 100% of these courses will transfer to almost any 4 year college or university.

Let's look at AAS and AOS degrees. I have a love hate relationship with these degrees, besides being the proud owner of one, I've taught in an AAS degree program for over 18 years. For the first 15 of those years, I didn't understand the limits of the degree and how it applied to the students I was teaching. Now that I completely understand, I respect that this degree has a place, but most students (certainly more than 99% of mine) have no idea about the limitations of an AAS/AOS degree.   An AAS/AOS degree essentially does not transfer anywhere. There are *courses* within that degree that may transfer (English, psychology, math, etc.) but none of the "meat and potatoes" of the degree will count toward a bachelor's degree in the typical way.

The majority of AAS/AOS degrees contain 12-15 general education courses. These courses, as required by your specific state, are not taught through the department that you are enrolled in. If, for instance, you are enrolled in a nursing program, your math course could come from the math department (will transfer) or the nursing department (won't transfer). Since students overwhelmingly prefer to take courses in their own department, they unknowingly undermine the transferability of their own degree. Beyond the 1215 required general education courses, the remaining 45+ courses will not transfer, and the student must earn 45+ new credits when they transfer. The student doesn't repeat, rather they have not taken the general education courses expected of an incoming student. So, essentially, they start from scratch. To be clear, you're going to have to earn 45+ general education credits that you would have otherwise been earned taken in an AA or AS degree.

AAS/AOS degrees are always "in" something. These are also called technical degrees, or career degrees. The industry term is "terminal degree" which indicates that any enrolled student intends to stop their education upon completion. In my experience, many students do stop, but most object to the idea of being forced to stop. In mine and my husband's cases, we had already worked successfully in our fields for a number of years before contemplating a return to college. Imagine our shock when we found out that we had to start from scratch.

Many fields ONLY offer degrees in an AAS or AOS format, there are no choices at that college. You may want to look around if the degree your teen is considering is linked to an AAS or AOS degree. Again, the degree is legitimate, but it is not going to transfer into a 4 year program. In the case of the program I teach for, our AAS degree takes 3 years to complete. Our students who wish to earn a bachelor's degree upon completion have an additional 3.75 years to go. That's nearly 7 years to complete a 4 year degree.

If your child must complete an AAS/AOS program here are some tips:

- All electives should be selected from the GENERAL EDUCATION courses. Double check with an advisor that the elective is in fact a general education course.
- Have your student take multiple CLEPs
  beyond what counts in his degree. Actually don't even worry if the CLEP will count toward this degree, the point is that the credit is sitting on a College Board transcript ready to use if and when the time comes. It is unnecessary to submit CLEP credit to your child's college if it doesn't count toward the degree, CLEP credit does

not have to be sent anywhere, and it won't expire for 20 years.

- Before making a final enrollment decision, contact no fewer than 5 professionals working in the field your child hopes to enter. These professionals shouldn't be entry level workers, rather mid-career professionals who have spent time working their way up beyond the entry level position. Discuss your education plans with them, and ask for their input. If they suggest alternative routes, give their advice sincere consideration.
- Confirm that the school is regionally accredited. Courses from a nationally accredited school are unlikely to transfer, even if they are general education.

Department matters
Know your alpha-numeric!

When you look at a college catalog, the college usually does NOT distinguish between courses in various AA/AS or AAS/AOS degrees. Courses may be listed alphabetically, by date, or by department. Are all science courses equal? How do you know? To the untrained eye, all courses with similar titles may seem similar. However, nothing could be further from the truth. All courses are absolutely distinguished, and this is done by their alphanumeric.

The alpha-numeric indicates the department and course number. ENG101 (English 101) means that the English department is offering the course, and it is course number 101. One hundred is the minimum (closest to 100) degree of difficulty to count toward the degree. ENG102 would be the second semester that follows ENG101, etc. Only departments that function inside the AA/AS departments are transfer courses.

AA/AS departments are staffed with faculty that holds master's degrees, and the courses are open to all students who have met the requirements. AAS/AOS degrees house all other departments and fall outside of this requirement. These instructors are not necessarily degree holders, but meet the requirements set forth by their own department. For instance, a truck driving course will be taught by a highly qualified truck driver, not someone with a master's degree in biology (and that's a good thing!)

The courses outside the AA/AS departments are not always open to the public, sometimes you have to be enrolled in the certificate or degree program, but other times the courses are open to anyone with an interest. This is where you must use caution.

Let's look at one college's nutrition course choices. These are actual courses taken from a community college course catalog.

Nutrition Table 1.0

COURSE NUMBER	COURSE TITLE	CREDITS	DESCRIPTION
NUT101	Introduction To Nutrition	3 CEU	A study of basic principles of human nutrition including classification of nutrients. Prerequisites: None
BIO210	Introduction To Nutrition	3	A study of basic principles of human nutrition including classification of nutrients. Prerequisites: BIO101
CUL210	Introduction To Nutrition	3	A study of basic principles of human nutrition including classification of nutrients. Prerequisites: CUL101

Let's evaluate the courses shown in the Nutrition Table 1.0

First, notice that they all share the same title, the same description, and for the sake of argument, let's assume they share the

69

same text book. For all intents and purposes, these courses are *exactly* the same. Are they?

In the first course, NUT101, the course is not for **actual** college credit. We can tell by the "CEU" written in the credit column. CEU stands for "continuing education units." This course is for professional or personal interest only, and the credit will not count for any degree offered at the college. It is possible that this course *could be* offered in a certificate program, or that it *could be* approved for ACE credit (see previous chapter) but with near certainty, this course will not be eligible for use in a degree.

The second course, BIO201 is actually taught through the biology department. We can tell by the BIO which means "biology." This course is an AA/AS or college transfer course because it is classified as a general education/transfer course. This is an ideal course to take. If you noticed a small clue, you'll notice that this course had a prerequisite from the biology department, clues like that can help you determine if a course is a general education course or not.

The final course, CUL210 is taught through the culinary arts department. We can tell by the CUL which means "culinary." This course is through an AAS/AOS degree, not an AA/AS degree program. This course will meet the degree requirements of an AAS/AOS degree only, not the requirements of an AA/AS. In addition, this course will likely NOT transfer to any 4 year college. Another clue is the prerequisite from the culinary department.

The bottom line is that the course title and content are not what makes the course transfer, it's the department. Whenever in doubt, always check with an advisor. As a general rule, departments that are considered AA/AS transfer (also called general education, or gen ed) include:

ENGLISH/LITERATURE
MATH/STATISTICS
BIOLOGY/CHEMISTRY
HISTORY
PSYCHOLOGY/SOCIOLOGY
FOREIGN LANGUAGE
COMPUTER SCIENCE

There are others, and there are exceptions, always check the college catalog. Clues to AAS/AOS or non-transfer include:
TECHNOLOGY (when attached to any title)
APPRENTICESHIP, CLINICAL, or PRACTICUM
CAREER, TRADE, or ASSISTANT in the title

Enrollment trumps employment
Colleges create majors because there is a demand from students.
Colleges do not create majors that they can't get enrollment for, regardless of the industry demand. College trends come and go. Television is a tremendous influence on college majors, especially forensics (CSI), anthropology (Bones), Psychology (Lie to Me), Legal (Law and Order), etc. Consider the spike in Air Force enlistments when Top Gun was a box office hit! The program I teach for

has had an unending request for baking courses (Cake Boss), so we are creating a baking program to meet the demand.

What's wrong with meeting the customer's demand? Unfortunately, many parents and students believe that all programs lead to employment. In other words, if there is an official degree program, there must be an accompanying career/job that you'll be qualified for. Sometimes that's not the case. Many times, it's not.

Let's consider a hypothetical degree was developed in Dish-washing. Perhaps the degree introduces the most sophisticated dish washing technology, a scientific study of alkaline soaps, a water chemistry course, and an internship to top it off. For 2 years, you've trained with the most advanced and brightest dish-washing faculty on the planet. Our graduates will be, literally, the highest educated dish-washers in the United States, from the only dish-washing degree program in the country.

Now what? Dish-washing, as a career, still pays minimum wage. The industry doesn't demand applicants hold dish washing credentials of any kind, let alone a degree, thus the credential doesn't make them a better candidate than someone walking in off the street. In addition, a potential employer may fear the over-qualified applicant will want more pay then they are prepared to give. That the applicant expects "more" out of the job. This candidate just reduced their chance of employment rather than enhancing it.

This story was hypothetical, but stories like it are very real. Community colleges and career schools are full of certificate and degree programs that produce poverty level workers, it's just a fact. I can count 27 programs offered at my college that pay less than $10 per hour. I can count more than that offered by our non-profit competition. If I include the for-profit inflated tuition options in my town, we've got more than 50. An 18 year old student doesn't fully understand how that relates when you have a family, or that there is little to no opportunity for advancement. If that student later decides to pursue additional education to counter this barrier, the young man (likely an AAS or AOS graduate) may not have many options except for starting over with little to no credit.

Is there anything wrong with simply following your dream? Of course not, but I'm for informed consent, and admissions advisors are not discussing the drawbacks and economic prospects of many programs. As mentioned in Chapter 1, the best preparation is to do your own research. Use the United States Department of Labor Occupational Handbook to find out the facts relating to training and salary for any field your child is considering. Providing wise council is a perk of parenting.

A final thought on degree yield, some fields require graduate degrees (master or doctorate) to practice. Psychology is an example of one of those fields. Psychology is currently the number 1 undergraduate major in the United States (Associate /Bachelor), followed by Business Administration. The fact remains, that there aren't employers waiting for psychology degree holders.   A student with a degree in psychology is certainly employable and educated; however, they have not yet been *trained* for anything specific. Unless a student is committed to continuing on to graduate school, you may consider persuading your child into a field with good employment potential. Weighing the decision between degree utility, and what you are interested in, is a big undertaking, and not to be considered lightly.

If your child insists on studying a subject that has little to no positive employment options, it is essential that they take on as little debt as possible. That's important advice for anyone, but a degree can cost more than a home, and responsible borrowing includes a plan for repayment. The use of CLEP exams, dual enrollment, summer courses, etc. can reduce the cost burden and keep the costs low. In this case, encourage your child to pay cash for college, reducing the debt burden that will rear its head 6 months after graduation. If following your dreams means a low paying career, debt will make the degree a curse rather than a blessing. (Hat tip to Dave Ramsey)

There's blood in the water.

In addition to college reps, there are a handful of other "helpful" people whose interest in your child isn't altruistic. Homeschooling, especially this decade, is exploding. And on the coat-tail of every explosion is a collection of entrepreneurs hoping to have a slice of the action.

Everything I'm sharing in this book is public knowledge, available for free. Many of the resources I'm sharing with you are also free. I've no financial interest in promoting one test over another or any study resource over another. In fact, I've written thousands of pages which are publicly viewable on the internet (Instant Cert Forum) to anyone at any time for free. I've spoken to homeschool groups (for free) and have even ushered a few other children, besides my own, through this process. It just so happens that I find testing and homeschooling fantastically interesting, and I enjoy helping others in the same way others have helped me. This is my hobby, and like most enthusiasts, I'm thrilled to share it with you.

My caution to you is this: if someone is selling testing information, selling a service to help you test, selling a counseling service, or promising your child college credit, RUN! Before you finish this book, you'll have all the tools you need to plan and implement a successful high school curriculum that will result in a lot of potential credit. At no time can ANYONE promise you that a college will award your child credit that is up to the specific college at the time of your child's application. Be highly suspicious of these companies, whom I will not advertise by naming names, and know that they are an unnecessary (and expensive) way of walking this journey.

While once upon a time we might have needed a travel agent to look up airfares, we can now do so easily. The same is true on this journey. Everything you need is in these pages, you won't need to hire a consultant or agent to help you work this process. Save your money!

HIGH SCHOOL PLANNING

Chapter 4 Resource Summary:

Home School Legal Defense www.hslda.org

CLEP College Board www.collegeboard.org

Advanced Placement www.collegeboard.org

DSST (DANTES) www.getcollegecredit.com

ALEKS Math www.aleks.com

High school is comprised of grades 9, 10, 11, and 12. In many states, you will be required to follow a course of study that may be mildly directed or very specific. Some parents use a credit system to determine when their child will graduate (example: the completion of 24 credits). Others will use the calendar, and others use the compulsory attendance laws in their state. You still may be undecided about which method to choose. Your method will largely be determined by your state's laws and your preference. No one system is always better than the next, but before looking too far ahead, be sure you have a solid understanding of your legal obligations.

As I've mentioned before, I strongly support the Home School Legal Defense Association. The HSLDA is a Christian organization, but you do not need to be Christian to belong. In fact, short of having a significant religious objection, I believe everyone should become a member family. The small yearly fee provides your family the legal oversight of the BEST HOMESCHOOL LEGAL MINDS in the world. They will advise your family, provide you with forms, and defend your family at trial. Their organization is unmatched. In addition, many of the lawyers are homeschooling dads too, so they really have good intuition about how to help homeschooling families. For anyone, member or not, you can visit their website for an overview of the laws in your state. You'll need to do this before you begin.

In this chapter, I'm going to help you plan a simple high school curriculum, but I cannot begin to meet the needs of every homeschool family in the United States! So, this chapter is not intended to make the decisions or plans for you, rather to teach you how to plan for your family. There is no "one right curriculum" out there, because if there were, then everyone would be using it! Even public and private schools disagree about the "best" curriculum. With that in mind, try not to be too legalistic in your planning. Make an outline and review it often. Be flexible, increasing or decreasing speed to match your child's progress. Finally, as I've stated before, don't let the goal of earning credit interfere with the joy of your family's homeschooling.

In addition, I realize it is likely the mother that will be doing the planning. If you have one of those rare children who would rather plan their own high school/college degree, then by all means empower them to do so. I've met several children who have aggressively and accurately completed their entire associate or bachelor's degree without any help of their parents. This is highly unusual, but if your child has this gift, simply hand them this book and step out of their way!

Subjects

The following subjects are typical for most high school plans.

English, 4 years

Math, 2+ years

Science, 2+ years

Social Sciences, 2+ years

Electives (driver's education, foreign language, physical education, computers, art, business, apprenticeship)

Even if your child does not have their sights set on college after high school, your curriculum can be written in a way that awards college credit during high school. If, at a later time, your child decides to pursue college, they have already earned some credit. Remember that CLEP scores are valid for 20 years! Also, there are hundreds of credits available to your high school student, and more earning options than slots in any degree. You simply won't be able to use ALL the credit shown in the tables, so pick what fits your child and don't attempt to do "everything" in this book.

1. Understand the courses that make up each subject and to match them against potential credit options. Not all subjects have corresponding credit options, so having this list handy gives you a good starting point.

2.   Start where your child is. If your child is struggling in math, the notion of completing Calculus 2 is setting the stage for problems. Stay the course where you are. If your child happens to achieve a level worthy of college credit, then celebrate that fact. Jumping over important developmental courses may be a mistake.

3.   Most of the exams require a solid ability to read at the college level. This means that above all else, English comprehension is the most important skill. English comprehension mastery should be the goal. For a child "not good in reading" most of the CLEP or other credit earning options will be incredibly difficult. For emphasis, the content may be easy, but he questions may be in sophisticated style with advanced vocabulary.

4.   Not everything must be for college credit. Home economics, a lost essential skill, doesn't have a credit-earning option; neither does Bible, P.E., Personal Finance, or Guitar. This doesn't mean that you should forgo this course for a credit-bearing course. Use the credit-bearing courses as available, rather

than building an entire curriculum only around what earns credit.

5.   You cannot duplicate credit. Passing an exam or course twice does not double your credit, and is not allowed. For instance, taking a dual enrollment MAT120 College Algebra course at your community college will duplicate the CLEP College Algebra exam. In the following table, pay attention to the words "or" or "and" in the credit earning options column.

6.   The decision to award college credit (or not) is ALWAYS up to the college you attend. You can't guarantee that everything you do now will fit perfectly into a plan 4 years away. That's okay.

Reading the tables

Notice a + symbol means "in addition to"
Notice the use of –or– indicates choosing one
Notice the use of –and– indicating two or
more
Notice the number ( ) indicates the credit
potential

LANGUAGE ARTS 21 potential college credits in high school	
High School Courses	**Credit Earning Option**
9th grade English + 10th grade English + 11th grade English + 12th grade English	CLEP English Composition (6) -**or**- Advanced Placement English Language and Composition (3) -**or**- Dual Enrollment Community College course English 101 (3) **and** Dual Enrollment Community College course English 102 (3)
American Literature + 2 or more years high school English	CLEP American Literature (6) **and** CLEP Analyzing and Interpreting Literature (6)
English Literature + 2 or more years high school English	CLEP English Literature (6) **and** CLEP Analyzing and Interpreting Literature (6)
Speech	DSST Principles of Public Speaking (3)

Notes on Language Arts

You'll notice 4 subjects (rows) in the language arts table. (English Composition, American Literature, English Literature, and Speech) Each row indicates non-duplicating credit earning opportunities. For instance, your child can complete the credits in row one, and row two, and row three, and row four. Your child may also choose to earn credit in only one row. In any case, these credits are distributed according to traditional guidelines, and show the best-case use.

The American and English Literature exams are "content-specific" and involve specific recall of works of literature and authors. These are considered "harder" in that you must memorize literature pieces, and will benefit from reading a great deal. In contrast, the Analyzing and Interpreting Literature exam is a comprehension exam in which there is no recall of authors or works. This exam may be considered "easier" in that a good understanding of the English language and solid reading ability is all that is needed.

Not all colleges accept the CLEP English Composition exam, however, I'll inject my opinion and suggest your child take ENG101 and ENG102 for dual enrollment credit at the local college or online. This is one instance where large volumes of college level writing will be incredibly helpful in future college courses.

NATURAL SCIENCE	
36 potential college credits	
High School Courses	**Credit Earning Option**
Biology	CLEP Biology (6) **-or-** Adv. Placement Biology (6)
Chemistry	CLEP Chemistry (6) **-or-** Advanced Placement Chemistry (6)
Astronomy	DSST Astronomy (3)
Geology	DSST Physical Geology (3)
Physics	DSST Principles of Physical Science (3) **-or-** Advanced Placement Physics B (6) **and** Advanced Placement Physics C (6)
General Science	CLEP Natural Science (6)
Environmental Science	DSST Environment and Humanity (3) **-or-** AP Environmental Science (3)

Notes on Science

You'll notice 7 subjects (rows) in the natural science table. Each row indicates non-duplicating credit earning opportunities. For instance, your child can complete the credits in row one, and row two, and row three, and row four, through row seven. Your child may choose to earn credit in only one row. In any case, these credits are distributed according to traditional guidelines, and show the best-case use.

In college science, you'll notice multiples of 3 credits (non-lab) and multiples of 4 credits (lab) when reviewing credits. Exam credits, like these in the table, usually count as NON-LAB credit. This does not reflect whether or not **you** gave your child a lab experience at home. Non-science majors can generally use more AP/CLEP/DSST science credit than science majors, because none of these courses generally count toward a science major's degree. Science majors generally need the courses and the labs.

What if your child wants to major in science? Take the AP, DSST, or CLEP exams anyway. Studying at the college level will help him greatly. Later, in college, he will have the ability to learn the material in much greater depth than if he were learning it for the first time.

Additionally, if your child passes a science exam, consider further study through dual enrollment. Use a college advisor for guidance.

MATHEMATICS 21 potential college credits	
High School Course	**Credit Earning Option**
Algebra 1, Geometry	None
Intermediate Algebra, Algebra 2, College Algebra	CLEP College Math (6) **-and-** CLEP or ALEKS College Algebra (3)
Trigonometry, Pre-Calculus	CLEP Pre-Calculus (3) -or- ALEKS Pre-Calculus (3) -or- ALEKS College Algebra with Trigonometry (3)
Calculus	Adv. Placement Calc. AB (3) **-or-** Adv. Placement Calc. BC (6) **-or-** CLEP Calculus (3)
Statistics	DSST Principles of Stats (3) **-or-** AP Statistics (3) -or- ALEKS Statistics (3)

Notes on Math

You'll notice 4 subjects (rows) in the math table. Each row indicates non-duplicating credit earning opportunities. With one exception (row one: Algebra 1, Geometry), your child can complete the credits in row two, and row three, and row four. Your child may also choose to earn credit in only one row. In any case, these credits are distributed according to traditional guidelines, and show the best-case use.

Though not equal to CLEP or AP, I'd suggest using ALEKS math as a credit earning option along with or instead of CLEP and AP. The down side of using ALEKS, is that only a handful of colleges will award credit for ACE Evaluated courses, but for the price, it's worth considering as a curriculum choice that offers potential credit. You can use ALEKS as your curriculum, and in addition to passing the ALEKS course, your child can take the corresponding CLEP or AP exam. Notice that the highest math shown is Calculus 1. If your child can complete Calculus 1 before the end of 12th grade, I'd suggest dual-enrolling at the local community college for Calculus 2 and beyond.

Some colleges strictly require you to complete math in sequence (Algebra before Calculus) in order to earn credit. Avoid this potential pitfall by scheduling the exams as the material is learned.

Statistics, though listed last in the table, can be taken at any time.

SOCIAL SCIENCE 45 potential college credits	
High School Course	**Credit Earning Option**
Social Studies	CLEP Social Science and History (6)
U.S. History	CLEP U.S. History 1 (3) **-and-** CLEP U.S. History 2 (3) **-or-** AP U.S. History(6)
Western Civilization	CLEP Western Civ. 1 (3) **and** CLEP Western Civ. 2 (3)
World History	Advanced Placement World History (6)
European History	AP European History (6) **-or-** DSST West Europe 1945 (3)
Vietnam History	DSST A History of the Vietnam War (3)
Civil War	DSST The Civil War and Reconstruction (3)
Middle Eastern History	DSST Introduction to the Modern Middle East (3)
Soviet Union	DSST The Rise and Fall of the Soviet Union (3)
Government	CLEP American Govt. (3) **-or-** AP Govt. Politics U.S. (3)

Notes on Social Science

You'll notice 10 subjects (rows) in the social science table. Each row indicates non-duplicating credit earning opportunities. Your child can complete the credits in rows one, two, three, and so on. Your child may also choose to earn credit in only one row. In any case, these credits are distributed according to traditional guidelines, and show the best-case use.

Some states, even those with very few guidelines, generally have a government or civics requirement at some grade. Many states ask you teach your state's history, and other may require nothing. Check your state's laws to learn if these courses are required.

Many courses in the social science area have extensive over-lap. This means, for example, that while your child is studying United States history, he will also study the Civil War. You'll notice there is a dedicated exam to the Civil War, so you may construct those two courses together for maximum return.

The study of history will always be somewhat multi-disciplinary. You'll notice that literature, especially American literature, fits perfectly alongside the study of early United States history. If you enjoy teaching through a timeline, be sure to take advantages of these overlapping units.

ELECTIVE COURSES 45+ potential college credits	
High School Course	**Credit Earning Option**
Foreign Language for 2+ years	CLEP Exam: French, Spanish, or German (6 to 12 credits) **-or-** Advanced Placement Exam: French, Spanish, German, Japanese, Latin, Chinese (6 to 12 credits) **-or-** New York Language Exam Fifty languages (16 credits)
Sociology	CLEP Intro. Sociology (3)
Music Theory	Advanced Placement Music Theory (6)
Psychology	CLEP Intro. Psychology (3)
Health / Sex Ed.	CLEP Human Growth and Development (3)
Introduction to Business	CLEP Principles of Management (3) **-and-** CLEP Principles of Marketing (3)
Computer Science	Advanced Placement Computer Science (3)
Economics	CLEP Macroeconomics (3) **-or-** Advanced Placement Macro. (3) **-and-** CLEP Microeconomics (3) **-or-** Advanced Placement Micro. (3)
Computer Applications	CLEP Introduction to Computing (3) **-or-** DSST Information Systems and Computer Applications (3)

Notes on Electives

You'll notice 9 subjects (rows) in the elective table. Each row indicates non-duplicating credit earning opportunities. Your child can complete the credits in rows one, two, three, and so on. Your child may also choose to earn credit in only one row. In any case, these credits are distributed according to traditional guidelines, and show the best-case use.

In reality, the use of electives is unlimited. Once you consider incorporating dual-enrollment options through a community college, your child can study anything that suits their interest!

Notes on politics and religion

Statistically, more than 80% of you reading my book hold strong political or religious views; it may even be why your family chooses to homeschool. For that reason, I'm sure you're wondering where these views come into play, and if they'll be challenged.

In my experience, exam companies try to be "vanilla" in their exams. In other words, they try to remain factual, non-bias, and structure exams around the key elements of a subject. CLEP, DSST, and AP do a decent job in this regard. If you choose to guard your child from exposure to extreme positions, your best bet for doing so is through choosing your own curriculum and using CLEP, DSST, or AP exams for college credit. For Christians, science curriculum from companies like Apologia will do an excellent job preparing your child for the CLEP, DSST, or AP exam.

In contrast, every college *class* will be run by an instructor with human bias and political opinions of their own. The degree to which it infiltrates the subject is called their "academic freedom." Academic freedom has merit, but the degree at which it is exercised by some teachers will be troublesome to many parents. These are college courses, generally taught to adults (over 18). In our case, we are using these courses for our children (under 18) so judgment should be used.

College courses in psychology and sociology are exceptionally left-liberal in political presentation. Religious courses do not necessarily teach adherence to a specific doctrine except when that colleges holds a religious position. (Catholic universities will generally, but not always, emphasize a pro-life and pro-marriage position in their sociology courses more so than a public community college which will be decidedly pro-choice). If your family is conservative, a CLEP exam is likely your best bet. If you'd rather enroll your child in a course, consider previewing the college textbook and syllabus first.

High School Template

The next few pages provide a sample template that can be used, but is intended more as a guide for planning your own child's courses. As you review these samples, keep in mind you may change your own plan as your child progresses. Only after you begin will you understand if you are on the right path. For some, this schedule would be incredibly complex. For others, it may be too simple. Use your own homeschool philosophy as your guide.

High School Planning Template. A credit-bearing exam follows courses with an (X) in the template. Notice some courses span two or more semesters before the exam is offered.

9th GRADE	
10 potential credits	
FALL	**SPRING**
English: *9th grade English*	English: *9th grade English*
Math: *Algebra 1*	Math: *Algebra 1*
Science: *Biology w/ Lab*	Science: *Biology w/ Lab* (X)
Social Science: *United States History 1* (X)	Social Science: *Civil War and Reconstruction* (X)
Elective: *French 1*	Elective: *French 2*
SUMMER	
Optional	

10th GRADE	
27 potential credits	
FALL	**SPRING**
English: *10th grade English*	English: *10th grade English*
Math: *Algebra 2 w/ Geo.*	Math: *Algebra 2 w/ Geometry* (X)
Science: *Astronomy* (X)	Science: *Physical Geology* (X)
Social Science: *United States History 2* (X)	Social Science: *American Government* (X)
Elective: *French 3*	Elective: *French 4* (X)
SUMMER	
Optional	

11th GRADE 21 potential credits	
FALL	**SPRING**
English: *11th grade English*	English: *11th grade English*
Math: *Pre-Calculus*	Math: *Pre-Calculus* (X)
Science: *Chemistry w/ Lab*	Science: *Chemistry w/ Lab* (X)
Social Science: *World History*(X)	Social Science: *World Govt.* (X)
Elective: *American Literature*	Elective: *American Literature* (X)

12th GRADE 27 potential credits	
FALL	**SPRING**
English: *Dual Enrolled- English 101* (X)	English: *Dual Enrolled- English 102* (X)
Math: *Statistics* (X)	Math: *Dual-Enrolled- Calc 1* (X)
Science: *Physics w/Lab*	Science: *Physics w/Lab* (X)
Social Science: *Western Civ. 1*	Social Science: *Western Civ. 2* (X)
Elective: *English Literature*	Elective: *English Literature* (X)

Final thoughts on high school planning

The additional summer sessions are optional, but if your child is motivated, it will dramatically speeds up their credit-earning potential. Whether summer sessions are done on a college campus, online, or at home, the use of summer for even 1 course will pay off greatly in the end. For the kids (or parents) who need a break, that's fine too! As your child starts to accumulate credit, don't worry too much (yet) about if or where it will fit into their college program.

Rather than specific degree planning, aim for generally accepted credit norms. In other words, earning a little credit in many areas will likely work better than earning too much credit in few areas. A good rule of thumb is to limit earning in a **specific subject** to 16 or fewer credits. In some cases, 16 credits may still exceed what is allowed by a college, but there is no restriction on what you require as a parent.

This list will work for most students:

English Composition & Literature, 3-12 cr.
Speech, 0-3 credits
Humanities & Fine Arts, 6-12 credits
Social Science (Psychology/Sociology) 6-12 credits
Social Science (History/Government) 6-12 credits
Natural Sciences/Lab, 3-8 credits
Computer Applications, 0-3 credits
Mathematics, 3-6 credits

BUILDING GOOD CURRICULUM

Chapter 5 Resource Summary:

Official CLEP Guide www.collegeboard.org
Official AP Guides www.collegeboard.org
Official DSST Guide
www.getcollegecredit.com
REA Guides www.rea.com
The Complete Idiot's Guides
www.idiotsguide.com
For Dummies Guides www.dummies.com
Netflix (Instant or rental) www.netflix.com
Annenberg Media www.learner.org
Khan Academy www.khanacademy.org
MIT Open Courseware http://ocw.mit.edu
Peterson's Practice Tests
www.petersons.com
Saylor Free Online Classes www.saylor.org

Building Good Curriculum

You'll notice this chapter isn't titled "Selecting Good Curriculum" because I don't believe that homeschooling is ever that easy. If it were simply a matter of curriculum, we'd all buy it, public and private schools would switch to it, and 250+ curriculum companies would go bankrupt.

In my experience as a learner, a homeschool parent, and a professional educator, I've discovered that there are not always easy solutions. What comes easy to some is confusing to others. Rather than becoming frustrated with this fact, home school parents get to embrace it. A cornerstone of homeschooling is being able to customize to the needs of your child. We all know group schools don't have the privilege of adjusting mid-stream.

I believe every teacher, at least early in their career, feels personal responsibility for the success of her students. Sadly, the calendar marches on, and so must the schedule. We all recognize when a student doesn't "get it" and we try to help them keep pace. But with apologies to my fellow educators, we all know the pace of the class is set by the slowest learners. The children who already "got it" are bored and need enrichment!

Homeschool parents know this better than anyone. If there is a dip in interest or a lag in test scores, homeschool parents take that personally. Every homeschool parent I've ever met goes out of their way to buy the best curriculum for their child.

Like group schools, we too have our limitations. Maybe we have multiple children (check), a variety of learning styles (check), limited access to resources (check), limited space (check), a limited budget (CHECK!), or something else that requires us to thoughtfully do the best we can do with what we have.

Like most of you, I've spent a good share of money on curriculum. I frequently buy used, and I frequently sell my unused. Over nearly 2 decades, I think I've used all of the major brands you can name, and dozens of lesser-known programs. I've seen companies come and go, and I've written plenty of my own curriculum guides through the years. You might call me a bit of a "curriculum junkie."

As such, I'm the first to admit that what works for someone today, might not work for them next year. What works for one child, might not work for the next. And ultimately, we must try to do what we can with what we have. When we spin out of control, we should try and refocus. Life might allow a period of student-directed learning, but later requires a more teacher-directed learning experience. This isn't scope and sequence; it isn't planning for a national one-size-fits-all. Instead it's looking at your curriculum in its entirety over 13 years. In the end, a curriculum that works for your family IS the best curriculum.

It is in that vein that I'm going to provide you with good sources for building your curriculum. Keep in mind that this list might look less traditional than you'd expect. We are not trying to keep our kids in high school; we are trying to get them into college level material. I also will provide a good balance between books and media. I like both, and I frequently use both. Hitting material from multiple sources sometimes makes the difference between "getting it" and "getting lost."

We are going to layer 6 resources to build a successful curriculum for every subject that you/your child attempts. I've used this formula with great success. These 6 layers form a substantial learning package that will take your child far and ahead of a high school workbook. The curriculum package that you prepare will be 90% student-led, leaving you with the responsibility of structuring their resources, monitoring progress, and directing their learning. Your responsibility will be to hold them accountable, and help locate additional resources if they need them.

I'm confident that when this basic approach is used, your child will be successful with every AP, CLEP, or DSST exam you ask them to take.

Building your curriculum in 6 layers:
CLEP / DSST / AP Official Guide
Subject specific college text book
Exam specific study guide
Subject specific study guide
Video Support
Practice exams

Layer 1
CLEP / DSST / AP OFFICIAL GUIDES
Before starting your journey, you'll want to purchase the official guides. The Official guides contain every exam outline, as well as a practice test representative of the types of question on the exam. These guides are telling you "straight from the horse's mouth" what your child needs to study. It is the final authority, and you'll want your own copy.

Many guides are published "for" CLEP, DSST, and AP tests, but only official guides are official. At the time of this printing, all guides could be purchased from the official websites (see resource listing at the beginning of this chapter). The prices for new, current editions are as follows:
CLEP Official Guide $25.00
DSST $25.00
AP: Official Advanced Placement Guides are not available for purchase; however you can visit the College Board website for a free online guide. In addition, old copies of the AP exams are sold through the official College Board bookstore, for roughly $25

each. Initially, you may find this helpful to assess your child's readiness.

Layer 2
SUBJECT SPECIFIC COLLEGE TEXT BOOK

If you've ever had to purchase a college text book, you've likely spent about $100-$200 on the "required" book. If you've ever "sold back" a textbook at the end of the semester, you've likely received back about $10-$20, only to turn around and see it "for sale" again for $75-$80. Text books generate a very profitable revenue stream for campus bookstores. You may not know this, but your college's bookstore is a for-profit business, even if the college is a non-profit entity.

For enrolled students, this is a nightmare. You used to be able to buy used books, or share books, even take a hand-me-down text book for years. With the speed press printing of digital technology, text books are being "updated" nearly every year, making the previous printing obsolete.

Sometimes nothing more than a few photographs have been "updated." Yes, instructors insist on the current edition. Many colleges, including the one I teach for, are transitioning to "custom editions" that the instructor has helped assemble from a dozen other text books. These editions have zero resale value, and are next to impossible to find used. They've got-cha.

We'll discuss buying text books later, but for now, let's discuss the obsolete textbooks. What happens to obsolete text books? They get thrown away. Yes, literally. A text that cost a student $250 in January may end up in the dumpster in May. I've rescued, literally, dozens of text books that have later been used for independent study, home school classes, and college exams. What I couldn't use, I've passed along. Before buying a text, you should investigate your local campus bookstores.

The bookstore managers are your point of contact. Go in person, don't call. Ask if they'll be throwing away any books at the end of the semester, and if you might have a few. Since the blatant waste of money upsets students, the manager may be a little shy about sharing with you. However, be discrete, be friendly, and ask more than once. Take any and every book they give you. Take what you can use, share or donate the rest. Visit all of the community colleges and universities in your area. You'll hit the jackpot if you're persistent. The "cleaning out" months at a college are April/May, and November/December.

If you don't find all that you need for free, you can turn to online auctions. A hot current edition might go for a few dollars less than your college bookstore, but a cold last-year's edition will go 1/3 the rack rate, and 2 editions back you're likely to walk away with the book and shipping for $5.00 How do you know what books will work? You don't have to over-think this, but you can always find a starting point on a college website. If your child is attempting the biology CLEP, that is course equivalent to Biology 101 and Biology 102. Fortunately, most colleges (especially community colleges) have their college bookstore online now. This allows you to type in the name of your class (Biology 101) and see what books your school requires for that semester. Remember, there is no "best" book for Biology 101, so we are only looking for a few options.

If you can't find a link to your college's bookstore, you can use the online bookstore at Ocean County College in New Jersey. I've used their online bookstore frequently.

Once you've obtained the title of a book for your "class" simply write down that book's title or ISBN number. The ISBN number is like a social security number, and it will take you directly to the exact title the first time. By typing the title or ISBN number into an online auction site, like eBay, you'll see the current book being used for Biology 101.

Here is a sample of what you might find when searching for a copy of a biology text:

(new, 2012) The Bios, 5th Ed. S. Sims $235.00
(used, 2012) The Bios, 5th Ed. S. Sims $200.00
(used, 2010) The Bios, 4th Ed. S. Sims $80.00
(used, 2006) The Bios, 2nd Ed. S. Sims $16.00
(used, 2000) The Bios, S. Sims $3.00

It would be funny if it weren't so sad. If I were choosing a book from the above list for my son's home-based biology course, I would likely choose the 2006 edition. It's less than 10 years old, so still very relevant. Short of breaking the DNA code and reclassification of Mars, you're generally fine using an older book. I likely wouldn't go with a book that was more than a decade old unless the subject was stable. For instance, if the subject were U.S. History prior to the Civil War, or College Algebra, you can bet I'd buy the $3.00 edition without hesitation. That information doesn't need updating every decade. In any case, just be happy your child isn't enrolled in the course that requires the 5th edition.

Layer 3
EXAM SPECIFIC SUBJECT STUDY GUIDES
These guides will generally say "CLEP" or "AP" in the title. They are designed to be summaries of courses, rather than a course itself. There are dozens of bad CLEP / AP /DSST guides out there. I'll skip the bad-mouthing and tell you who the best is.
REA (Research and Education Association)
REA is seriously, the best of the best. Start with REA if it is available. Not all subjects have REA guides, but enough do that it's really where you should begin. REA offers study guides, extremely concentrated information into a single book. REA guides all include practice exams, and a key to help you assess how close you are to readiness on your CLEP or AP exam. These guides mirror

the study outline that The College Board has specified for their exams.

REA offers books specifically for both CLEP and AP, and while the exam content is nearly the same, if you have to option you might choose the one for the test you plan to take. In a pinch, however, you can use them interchangeably with slight modification. REA guides have recently started to offer CD-ROMs; however, my limited experience with these has been lukewarm. They are redundant of the text and cost extra, plus they may or may not work on your computer. At the end of the day, the book is all you need.

REA guides are also exceptional for as long as the exam content remains unchanged. The College Board occasionally revises exams, but not very often. With confidence, I can suggest to you that any REA book published within the past 10 years will do a good job of preparation.

For this reason, scour your local library and online auction sites for used copies. I've even found a library discard REA (25 cents thank you very much) that I later used to test out of a $750 class.

If you must buy new, consider creating a share group with 1 or 2 other CLEP-AP minded homeschool families. If each of you purchased 2 books for the "group library" you'd have a nice collection to share amongst each other. Used, expect to pay $15 for a current (+/- 5 years) REA guide. New, expect to pay around $35.00

REA guides specifically for CLEP/AP tests:
American Government (CLEP, AP)
American Literature (CLEP)
Art History (AP)
Biology (CLEP, AP)
Calculus (CLEP, AP)
Chemistry (CLEP, AP)
College Algebra (CLEP)
College Composition/English (AP, CLEP)
College Math (CLEP)
English Literature (AP)
Environmental Science (AP)
European History (AP)
Financial Accounting (CLEP)
General Exam Group (all 5 General CLEP)
History of the US 1 (CLEP)
History of the US 2 (CLEP)
Human Growth and Development (CLEP)
Humanities (CLEP)
Information Systems Computer Applications
Introductory Sociology (CLEP)
Macroeconomics (CLEP, AP)
Microeconomics (CLEP, AP)
Natural Sciences (CLEP)
Physics (AP)
Pre-Calculus (CLEP)
Principles of Management (CLEP)
Principles of Marketing (CLEP)
Psychology (AP)
Social Science and History (CLEP)
Statistics (AP)
United States History (AP)
Western Civilization 1 (CLEP)
Western Civilization 2 (CLEP)
World History (AP)

Once you have an REA guide, locate the tests. Try to cover or fold them away and avoid the temptation of looking at them ahead of time. Even a quick peek makes your child's results unreliable; they'll be plenty of time to test later.

REA books have a wonderful timeline in the front of each guide. They direct your learning into about a month or two in preparation for a test. Since you'll likely be using the guide over the course of semester or full year, you may want to review but disregard that outline.

The guide will cover all of the major areas necessary, but because of the condensed nature of the guide, it will likely NOT be sufficient to learn the subject. I like to say there is material you have to learn, and there is material you have to know. REA guides show you what you have to know for the test. You'll be grateful later for the ability to zone in on what's important. However, you'll still need to fill out the semester will resources, labs, media, web, and homework. I'll help you do this over the next few pages.

Layer 4
SUBJECT SPECIFIC STUDY GUIDES

My two favorite subject-specific study guides are *The Complete Idiot's* series and the *Dummies* series. Both do a nice job a brining the subject out of academia and to the average reader. Remembering that our high school teen may not fully comprehend everything they are reading in their college text books, so this is a good filter that helps paint a nice picture of what they need to understand.

The Complete Idiot's Guides

I've used Idiot Guides with much success, and they are readily available at most libraries. What makes this resource unusual is that they don't specifically prepare you for a college level course or college level exam. You won't find an Idiot's Guide for the American Literature CLEP. You will find, however, that their guide to American Literature is superior to any American Literature resource out there. It even beats REA and a college text discard. It's beautifully and humorously written, and mirrors the CLEP exam almost to the letter. The Complete Idiot's Guides have an informal-conversational tone that makes even the most complicated subjects very approachable. The depth of these guides is likely NOT enough to prepare for an exam alone. But when combined with the other resources in this chapter, it really rounds out an excellent curriculum plan.

Expect to find The Complete Idiot's Guides as library discards, at garage sales, in libraries for loan, used for about $10, and new for about $17.00

There are about 500+ Complete Idiot's Guides, but this short list is most relevant to your high school curriculum:

Algebra
American Government
American History
American Literature
Calculus
Civil War
English Literature
European History
Foreign Language (40+)
Geometry
Middle Eastern Hist.
Pre-Algebra
Pre-Calculus
Statistics
U.S. Govt. /Politics
Vietnam War
World History

For Dummies Guides

These guides are the competing brand to the Complete Idiot's Guides. Like Idiot's Guides, you'll find these easily in many libraries and garage sales.
Here is a short list of the most relevant titles:

Art History
Astronomy
Biology
Biology Workbook
Calculus
Calculus Workbook
Foreign Language
Geology
Geometry
Geometry Workbook

Latin
Middle East
Pre-Calculus
Pre-Calculus Workbook
Psychology
Sociology

Layer 5

VIDEO & MEDIA SUPPORT

Sometimes, it just takes someone explaining something for it to click. I have found a handful of excellent "teachers" who are available to help your child understand a subject. With internet access now in nearly every home, most of these resources are simply a click away.

Undoubtedly, I've left out the thousands of relevant documentaries on Netflix or clips on Youtube, but I'll let you discover those for yourself. My (much shorter) list is a collection of the tried and true sources you can count on completely.

These three sources are the best of the best, plus one extra source I'm excited about. You'll be able to find everything you need at the following 3 sites, but don't let that discourage you from branching out.

As I type this, MIT's continuing education division announced a new innovative program which will offer online courses completely free to anyone who signs up. These courses will even offer certificates. In addition to our high school students having the option of "attending" MIT at home, they can soon use those courses (which do not provide college credit) to prepare on their own for exams like CLEP or AP which will provide college credit. I expect this move will stir up competition among the top tier colleges; we are undoubtedly on the brink of an information access revolution! It is truly an extraordinary time to be a homeschooled child in America!

Use one or more of these FREE online video courses to complement your layered curriculum. At the risk of being too broad and shallow, select one course and go with it. Information overload can be time consuming and not necessarily helpful.

RESOURCE 1: Annenberg Media
www.learner.org

Against All Odds (AP / DSST statistics)

Algebra in Simplest Terms (CLEP Algebra)

Art of the Western World Series (DSST art)

Art Through Time (CLEP Humanities)

Discovering Psychology (AP/CLEP Psych)

Economics 21st Century (AP / CLEP Micro and Macro Economics)

French in Action (AP /CLEP French)

Neuvos Destinos (AP / CLEP Spanish)

The Habitable Planet (DSST Environment)

The Mechanical Universe (Physics)

RESOURCE 2: Khan Academy
www.khanacademy.org

Algebra (CLEP College Algebra)

Art History (DSST Art of the Western World)

Astronomy (DSST Astronomy)

Biology Series (CLEP or AP Biology)

Calculus (CLEP Calculus)

Chemistry Series (CLEP or AP Chemistry)

Economics (CLEP Macroeconomics & CLEP Microeconomics)

Physics (CLEP Physical Science or AP Physics)

Statistics & Probability (DSST Statistics)

RESOURCE 3: MIT Open Courseware
http://ocw.mit.edu

Anthropology (DSST Anthropology)

Biology (CLEP or AP Biology)

Chemistry (CLEP or AP Chemistry)

Economics (CLEP Microeconomics CLEP Macroeconomics)

Political Science (CLEP American Govt.)

RESOURCE 4: Saylor Foundation
www.saylor.org

*At the time of this writing, Saylor is in progress creating extensive amounts of free curriculum in addition to courses aligned specifically to CLEP, DSST, and AP exams. I have limited information about Saylor at this time, but expect wonderful things from them!

Art History

Biology

Business

Chemistry

Communications

Computer Science

Economics

Literature

History

Math

Mechanical Engineering

Layer 6
PRACTICE EXAMS

Not everyone uses practice exams as a curriculum tool, but I find them extremely useful. In addition to providing peace of mind ("am I really ready?") it exposes your child to questions in several ways. For instance, a text book frequently asks questions tied to their reading material. Sometimes it's even "word for word" which isn't helpful. Being able to understand what is being asked is an important test taking skill, more so than being able to memorize questions in your text. Without apology, I recommend only two test brands: REA and Peterson's.

REA Tests

REA, as you may recall, publishes study guides. These study guides, besides being excellent, include three practice tests in each guide. These tests, if anything, tend to be a click harder than the real exam, but the genius is in their answer guide. Most practice tests (including the College Board Official CLEP guide) only provide you with a correct answer. REA guides actually provide explanation for each answer. Many times, understanding the reason an answer is correct, is as important as knowing the answer.

REA guides provide a score converter, which is designed to give you an expected test result. If you score X on their practice test, you can expect a certain score on the real CLEP exam. I'd caution you against giving this too much credibility. The real CLEP/AP/DSST test banks are randomized, so your test and mine will differ slightly. If your child has an excellent understanding of a particular area, their score can be influenced by an unusually high number of those questions....or an unusually low number of those questions.

If REA exams are not available, you can rely on Peterson's (discussed in a moment) or use an alternative brand. Since my experience with alternative brands is inconsistent, I'll simply remain silent on that issue.

As your child completes their REA exams, you'll need to find an exam percentage. Simply take their score (number right) and divide by the total number of questions. Move the decimal two places to the right, and that is their score represented as a percentage.

My score: 48
Total number of questions: 90
48 divided by 90 = .53333
Move the decimal two places to the right: 53.3%

After every test, you should notice an upward trend. It is reasonable for your child's first few tests to be under 50%. In fact, you may see early results around 20%. Don't be alarmed. The subjects are vast, and learning takes time. Again, the goal is an upward trend. 20% last week and 30% this week is good and a move in the right direction. When your child is earning greater than 50% on REA and Peterson's exams, they are probably ready. If your child can score greater than 60% on more than one test, I can suggest with high confidence that they will pass their exam if taken immediately.

To keep the results pure, do not have your child retake the same test twice as tests as a measuring tool. You can retake a test as a study tool, but after taking the test once, it is no longer valid as a means of measuring readiness. Stated again, retaking the same exam IS NOT A RELIABLE assessment of readiness.

Peterson's Tests

Peterson's tests are offered electronically, and a few are also available to print off and take paper based. Peterson's tests are retail priced at $20, and include 3 electronic tests (instantly scored). Some offer a printable version, (ie. Biology offers this feature) which is great, because this is a 4th exam at no extra charge. These are notoriously more difficult than the "real" exams, so scoring well on Peterson's is an excellent measure of your child's readiness. For $20, your child will have online access to the exams for 90 days. Since this is usually not long enough for an entire semester, don't register until your child is nearing the end of your class. You'll want to allow plenty of practice time before the real exam.

There are many resources available for finding free or reduced fee access to this brand of tests. Your local library, or libraries in your state, sometimes buy access to a portal and make this portal available to its patrons for free. Members of the military and veterans also can usually access these portals for free. This process can sometimes be via special pass code, library card, or other means. It's ethically questionable for me to share a list of these portals, but be aware of their existence and certainly inquire at your own library. If they are unwilling to provide free access, you can request that they consider funding a portal in the future. Doing so is an excellent service to the community, especially if your community includes a large number of homeschooled children who will be attempting CLEP/AP/DSST exams.

Like REA exams, don't expect high scores initially. What you should expect to see is an upward trend. The Peterson's tests will calculate the percentage for you, and it is instantly displayed upon the completion of a test. Similarly, multiple scores nearing or exceeding 60% are excellent indicators of readiness.

Now that you have a guide for building the 6 layers of your curriculum, the opposite page can be used as a template for EACH course you plan to offer for credit.

6 Layers of curriculum

CLEP / DSST / AP Official Guide
Subject specific college text book
Exam specific study guide
Subject specific study guide
Video Support
Practice exams

Additionally, remember not all courses need to award college credit, but many high school courses "nearly" prepare your child anyway. On the other hand, if a course you've planned starts out well but declines beyond recovery, you can still use it for high school credit. Simply cancel the exam. Before creating individual courses, you may wish to plan (even temporarily) an overall high school plan covering all four years.

The COURSE PLANNING TEMPLATE, will help you create a single course by assembling 6 layers of curriculum. Photocopy each template as often as needed.

COURSE PLANNING TEMPLATE

COURSE: _____

TEST: _____

Passing Score: _____

High School Credit:_____

College Credit Possible:_____

Course Start Date: _____

Course End Date:_____

Testing Date:_____

Testing Center Location and Phone Number:

_____

_____

Contact Person:_____

Fees / How to Pay:_____

Types of I.D. required _____

RESOURCE NEEDED	TITLE TO BE USED	√
Layer 1 Official Guide		
Layer 2 Subject Specific Text Book		
Layer 3 Exam Specific Study Guide		
Layer 4 Subject Specific Study Guide		
Layer 5 Video Support		
Layer 6 Practice Exam		

When you have filled out your COURSE
PLANNING TEMPLATE, you can then create a
weekly guide for the course, known as the
COURSE SYLLABUS. This week-by-week
lesson plan should work for you, you
shouldn't be a slave to it! On the other hand,
it may provide a sense of urgency to remain
organized, and stick to a schedule.

COURSE SYLLABUS planning tips:

Text Book- Rarely would your read an entire text book in one semester. Many subjects, like science, expect the text book to be used for a 2-part course, in other words, over an entire year. In most cases, you'll find the first 2/3 of the text contain the most important information for the subject, while the last 1/3 contain less relevant material. Feel free to skip irrelevant chapters.

Subject Study Guides- Sometimes so tightly condensed, that they don't neatly match a test 1 chapter for 1 chapter. For example, chapter 1 in the study guide may match chapters 1-4 of your text.

Exam Study Guides- Like subject study guides, these are going to strip away everything except the essential core knowledge. Personally, I like to save these until the last few weeks and use them to "hammer home" the relevant points. How you use the guides is up to you, and can simply accompany the text at relevant chapters.

Video Titles- I would allow your student some flexibility in the use of videos. Sometimes, a video is a great way to get you "unstuck" on a topic (Khan Academy!) while others do a better job of helping you understand the topic more casually (Annenberg Media). I generally assign a video or two each week, but I encourage my child to use the videos as they need.

HOW TO TAKE A TEST

Chapter 6 Resource Summary:

Locate a CLEP /AP testing center, The College Board www.collegeboard.org

AP Test taking tips, The College Boardwww.collegeboard.org

Locate a DSST testing center, official DSST Sitewww.getcollegecredit.com

Instantcert www.instantcert.com

Forum at Instantcert www.degreeforum.net

You've applied the 6-layer technique to your curriculum, and you're nearing the end of the semester. Around week 14 (if you're following the outline) you'll have completed the bulk of learning and begin the final two weeks of test preparation. Those final two weeks involve finishing your practice exams, reviewing the mistakes you made, and scheduling your actual exam. This chapter walks you through more details about how to use those final two weeks, and what you'll need to do on exam day. Let's briefly review the two types of tests your child will take. You may still be undecided about which exam to register for (AP vs CLEP/DSST). This chapter should help you decide.

Advanced Placement exams (AP)

An Advanced Placement exam is the brand commonly offered at the end of a high school Advanced Placement course. High schools typically offer AP courses/exams only to the top students in a class. As such, more than 90% of high school students never even know that this credit-earning option is available to them.

As a homeschool family, you'll independently prepare your child for the AP exam. At the conclusion of the school year, your child can sit the exam with their peers at a local school. Since AP and CLEP are created by the same company, the exam material is nearly identical. You can use the test-prep material interchangeably. AP exams will require an essay, so additional practice in writing will be required.

Local high schools vary in the AP courses they offer their students, so unless a school offers the course your child is taking, they probably won't be offering the exam. If your child is taking a common exam like calculus, you may have multiple schools to choose from. A more obscure exam, like Latin, may only be offered 50 miles away! This is why you must plan ahead. Even freshman year is not too soon to collect a list of AP classes offered at your local high schools.

If you're using an AP exam, be aware that you will not get to schedule the exam. The school will set your test day and time for you. AP exams happen over a week or two, so be sure your child has reliable transportation well ahead of time. Retakes are almost impossible.

Finally, each high school that offers AP courses has an AP coordinator. This person should be your point of contact. They will reserve your child's place on exam day, discuss the itinerary for test week, and arrange to receive payment. On a side note, AP coordinators are the gate-keepers. They can refuse to allow your homeschooler access to the exam, so be friendly. On the other hand, you have the option of contacting more than one school.

The testing center at a high school will likely consist of a desk or table in a large space like a library or gymnasium. The format will be pencil/paper. The exam proctor will be a teacher with proctoring certification. AP teachers are never AP proctors. Expect some confusion and chaos as these tests are only given once per year. Expect your child to be in a group environment, and the distractions that come with it. A photo ID will be required, and items like food, water, pens, calculator, phones, etc. will be strictly regulated. Do not assume anything is allowed in the testing space. Violating a testing center policy can cause your exam score to be void.

Your exam will receive a score ranging from 1-5. 3 is considered "passing" and 5 is considered exceptional or highly proficient. Most colleges that award credit will do so for scores 3 or above. Before settling on an AP exam, compare the college's policy for CLEP. If the college is more generous with CLEP credit, choose CLEP over AP. Some colleges simply like CLEP better than AP, while others like AP better than CLEP. You'll likely discover this as you start to compare colleges. (See chapter 2 for additional AP test information)

CLEP/DSST exams

CLEP and DSST testing centers and formats are very similar, and I'll address them interchangeably. They are two different brands that complement each other nicely. Both offer subjects that their competition doesn't, so if one doesn't work, the other one probably will. CLEP and DSST exams are both multiple choice exams. They are given on a computer with a timer at an official testing center. A testing proctor will be present during the exam.

It's likely that your local center will be a college or military base. In both cases, a variety of exams are given for a number of reasons, so these testing centers will be a little more organized and efficient than an AP exam at a high school. Your work station will be at a computer, and you will be given scratch paper. If you are not, you must request it from the exam proctor. The room will likely be small, perhaps with as few as 2-3 work stations up to a dozen. Like AP, expect heavily regulated policy regarding food, drinks, phones, back-packs, etc.

I tend to favor CLEP/DSST over AP except in a few specific situations. Ultimately, convenience wins for me. When you plan to take a CLEP/DSST, you set the date and time. If you fail an exam, you can re-take it in 6 months. Neither option is available for AP. CLEP/DSST lends itself to a homeschool family's high school schedule very well; even if your family uses a unit approach (1 subject at a time). The unit study approach won't work for AP due to schedule restrictions.

Count-down to test day

As you approach the test day, use your practice exams as a measure. We spoke before about how the practice exams can be harder than the real thing, but the results should still be trending upward. If your child is not performing to your expectation on the practice tests, you need to find out why. The deficiency is either with content, or with testing acumen.

Content

Just because you have great material, doesn't mean it's all locked away in your brain. We forget things! Exams require recall, and sometimes that's difficult. Once issue with recall, is that our study resources taught us a lot of material. We have a "global" understanding of the topic without an ability to recall specific "details" in the subject. I'm compassionate to those students, because I share that tendency. If your child can talk endlessly about the subject but isn't scoring well, can't recall specific facts or dates, then suspect this to be the case. The cure for this deficiency is Instantcert (see resource list at beginning of chapter). Instantcert may ring a bell; I mentioned it in my opening Acknowledgements of this book. I owe a great debt to Instantcert! Instantcert is a website that has created study material for nearly every CLEP/DSST (and other) exams. They use a flash card method. The genius of the site is that the material on each card is directly tied to the exams. There's nothing bogging down your learning with unnecessary information.

Instantcert is best suited for adult learners or students who have studied the material. It isn't intended to replace a high school curriculum. For that reason, I recommend it as a supplement. Instantcert costs $20 per month. An additional perk to members, is access to the forum. Forum access is free, but Specific Exam Feedback is not. Aside from the forum being my "home away from home" I love the Specific Exam Feedback section. This is a free exchange of ideas from students who've just taken the exam you are preparing for. Hearing guidance and suggestions from peers is invaluable. I highly suggest checking out both resources. *and if you do, be sure to send me a hello!

If the issue is not with details and recall, it may be with the subject. For any number of reasons, sometimes a subject is especially hard for some people. It could be that the material is miles over their head, the reading level is too high, their learning style isn't being met, or one of a million other things. In this case, all is not lost. I'd still suggest trying Instantcert for a month. See if using the flash card method brings your child up close to passing scores on their practice exams. If it doesn't, you can continue to deduce what the problem is, but at the end of the day, you can also decide to skip the test. Remember that skipping the test does not void the class! Your child still completed a semester of high school college-prep credit! The test, if taken and passed, is frosting.

Testing acumen

We all know people who "test well" no matter the subject, and without much studying. It's not really that they are smarter, but they have what I call **testing acumen.** They probably have learned the material, but they have *mastered* the art of testing.

There is an art to testing! CLEP and DSST exams are all multiple choice. The good news is that the answers are provided! They are right before your eyes. You just have to choose it. This isn't to say that some questions aren't tricky, they are, but knowing how to improve your testing acumen yields more of an increase than learning more facts. That said, these tips assume the student has *already studied* the material.

1.   Obtain the test content outline from the Official CLEP/DSST study guide.

2.   After joining Instantcert, read the Specific Exam Feedback information for your exam.

3.   Trust the first two suggestions. If CLEP/DSST study guide or a former test taker tells you to expect many questions about a topic, expect many questions about that topic! Know it well!

4.   Focus your study sessions on topics that dominate the exam. For instance, if one topic represents 25% of the exam, while another represents 3%, don't even bother reviewing or learning the 3% section. 3% of a CLEP/DSST exam amounts to no more than 2 questions. The odds of you studying the correct content in those two questions is astronomically low, that you'd be wasting precious study time doing so. 25%, on the other hand, is the difference between a pass and a fail.

5.   Know the basics inside and out. Knowing random "trivial pursuit" answers is not what the CLEP/DSST exams are about. They are testing your freshman/sophomore understanding. Do you know the basics covered in a college level course?

6.   Always understand why you missed a question and understand why you got it right. Read this sample question:

An example of a secondary color is:
   a.   Red
   b.   Blue
   c.   Yellow
   d.   Green

Since we know that the primary colors are red, blue, and yellow, we can deduce that "D" Green must be the answer. This question teaches us two clues, that we must know both primary and secondary colors for the tests.

7.   Read the question, understand the question. The placement of a period, a comma, or negative words (which one is not, which one except, etc.) all change the meaning. In this case, you'd miss a question that you potentially knew the answer to!

8.   Several questions have choices that include more than one good answer, but one will always be the best answer. When in doubt, pick one and move on. In this case, if you feel that you have narrowed it down, and given it a moment of thought, then

spending 4 precious minutes agonizing only eats your time. Answer it, "mark it" and move on.

9.   If you don't know a question, answer it and then "mark it" for later. CLEP/DSST exams feature "mark" options which allow you to revisit questions later. Sometimes, a question or answer helps lend information in another question. This has helped me more than once!

10.   STAMINA! Exams last 90 minutes, and unless you've practiced concentrated test taking for 90 minutes, you'll be caught off guard at how hard it can be. In addition to using the clock for practice exams, know that your fatigue can get the best of you. While you won't be able to leave the room, you can close your eyes for 10 seconds and take a deep breath. Clearing your head and regaining focus can carry you through.

Brain Dump

Brain dump is a term that has bounced around Instantcert forum for years. Some exams require you to keep track of certain facts that you may have a hard time remembering. Perhaps you are trying to memorize amendments, or certain dates are giving you trouble. A "brain dump" is when you study up until the moment you must enter the testing center door. At that point, you'll sign in, pay, and go to your work station. Nothing can go into your test with you, but the tricky dates are still fresh in your mind.

At the moment you begin your exam, use your scratch paper and the first 2-3 minutes to "dump" all of the facts you hope to keep straight. In my case, I wrote out several dates and court cases that I feared mixing up later! Then, put it aside, and take your test. As you get into the test, you can continue to use your scratch paper, and if you need to recall dates/court cases/etc. they are there for you to use. You will have to turn in your scratch paper after your exam, but this method is completely legal.

Just before the test

You'll have to pay a fee to the testing center and testing company before you begin. Of the 6 testing centers I've used, all 6 had a different policy and procedure for payment. It is very important to call well ahead of your exam day and find out all you need to know. Find out the fees and how fees should be paid. Some require electronic (credit/debit) payment while others require check or cash. Some don't accept cash! You also need to find out about parking, guest or day passes, location of testing center, hours, rules, necessary identification, etc. For the parents, please accompany your child to their exam. As a minor, they may need your signature or ID but you'll have to wait outside during the exam.

When the proctor seats you at your computer, be sure you are comfortable. If the chair is broken, you're next to a wall with construction banging on the other side, or the room is freezing, ask for assistance. You've studied and paid a good fee to sit this exam, there are certain things you can expect as a consumer. It's not reasonable to have a private space, but you should have an adequate space with enough room to write on your scratch pad or use a calculator. In addition, if the room is so noisy that you won't be able to do your best, you can ask for a different time slot.

The proctor will help you get signed in to the computer. The exam is going to be streamed to the testing center; it isn't "on" the center's computer. As such, internet issues can and do occur. Remember, even a computer malfunction can void your exam, so if you notice anything at all, bring it to the attention of the proctor immediately. As you get signed in, you'll need to enter your full name, social security number, birthday, etc. When you are logged in, the proctor will leave and you may begin.

The initial few pages will ask you demographic questions. These are purely for statistical collection and have nothing to do with your test. Then, the exam will ask you if you'd like to have your exam scores sent to a college or institution. As a high school student, you simply select "no." I bring this up, because I've heard people worry that if you're not enrolled in college, that you can't test.

That's completely false. There are no age or college enrollment criteria for any of the CLEP/DSST exams. (This is not to say that some testing centers are limited to only their enrolled students. If this is the case, use The College Board website to find a different testing center that is open to the public.)

During the exam

Answer every question! There is no penalty for guessing, but an unanswered question will be wrong 100% of the time. An answered question still has a slight chance of being correct. Some tests are generally completed quickly, and some tests are notorious for taking the entire 90 minutes. I have a trick that I've used several times to assure no question goes unanswered.

If you are going to "mark" a question and come back to it, answer it first. Even if you just mark "A" without feeling certain about the answer, it will be answered in the event that you run out of time or forget to go back later.

At the half-way point (45 minutes) be sure you are half way through the questions. If you're not, don't panic. Just remember not to spend too much time on answers you do not know. Mark "A" (or B, C, etc.) and move on.

As you near the last 10 minutes of your time and still have many questions left, quickly mark "A" (or B, C, etc.) for all the remaining answers. While it's not scientific, I always feel that my odds are better if I pick one letter and mark it on every question. After all remaining questions are answered (A, A, A, A, etc.), go back to the question you left off on, and now answer the questions for real. You can enter in the correct answer as you go. If you run the clock out until the last minute, at least all of the answers were answered. I've used this tip on every exam that took me a full 90 minutes!

After the exam

For some reason, the exam companies give you the option to "cancel" your score. I've never understood the logic of this feature. If you don't pass, no one will ever know. Simply, your official transcripts from The College Board only contain exams you passed. So there simply isn't a valid reason to ever cancel a score. Cancelling a score means that you will not see your results, you do not get a refund, and you still must wait 6 months to attempt the exam again! Don't do it!

Despite this, as you submit your last answer, the computer will ask you if you'd like to cancel your score. It will then ask you if you're sure. And then even one more time if you're sure. It's more than a little anxiety provoking! After you've answered, your score will be displayed instantly on the screen. Next to your score will be the "passing score." If you scored equal or greater than the passing score, you've passed! Ask your proctor for a print out of your score report before you leave. If you take enough exams, or know people who do, you'll hear stories of failed exams. I've even failed one! It happens. Despite my encouraging words, you'll be upset and likely very bothered. Try to remember that many subjects are broad, and the test bank of questions is random. Sometimes, on that day, you just got questions you hadn't known. With tongue in cheek, I've always said "I hope they ask me the questions I know." And sometimes, it's just luck that they do, or just bad luck that they don't. In any event, if you really want the credit, you can re-test in 6 months. If this was an elective (or especially torturous) you should just chalk it up as a learning experience and move forward. I'd suggest retaking anything in math that you can count toward your degree or prerequisite, and any foreign language. Foreign languages award more credit than anything else, so the risk-reward is the highest!

You passed! Now what?

Congratulations! It's a wonderful feeling to earn college credit, especially if you're still in high school! Well, great job. The good news about your score is that it will be "saved" for 20 years. So, even if you take time off after college, it won't be lost. When the time comes that you'd like to collect all of your scores and submit them to a college, you will submit 1 transcript request form

($20) and they will mail your scores to the school(s) of your choice. You do not pay per exam you took; you only pay 1 transcript fee. In addition, failed exams are not included.

Remember, credit earned is technically only "potential credit." Even credit earned at another college isn't always a guarantee. In the end, the institution you earn your degree from will ultimately make the decision as to how much credit you receive. If you ever transfer, your credit is subject to re-evaluation by the new school you intend to earn a degree from.*

As such, you can (and should) shop various colleges to see who will award you the most credit for your hard work. You'll be surprised at the differences!

there is an exception to the re-evaluation rule. If you complete an AA/AS degree through a school that has an official transfer agreement (articulation agreement) with a 4-year college, then your AA/AS degree transfers as a "block" of credit and each individual credit is not re-evaluated. This method allows you to choose a community college with maximum CLEP-friendliness and thus jump over the university's CLEP policy. Before attempting this strategy, be certain you are enrolled in an articulation agreement.

Final thoughts on testing

Homeschool kids are generally less tested than group school kids, it's just the nature of our education system. That doesn't mean that they'll test poorly or have trouble with

CLEP exams. If, however, your child is especially nervous, be sure they've taken numerous practice exams ahead of time. You can also visit the testing center a few days before. Once your child gets his first "pass" under his belt, he'll be on the path to success. When I first considered if my son would take a CLEP exam, I decided to try one myself. I wondered what they were like, how hard they were, and if they really were something we could include in our homeschooling. If you're willing, I strongly encourage you to take an exam first. In addition to giving you tremendous insight, you'll simply be better assimilated to the process. As a result, you'll be a better guidance counselor. Test suggestions for a mom? Try CLEP's Human Growth and Development. It covers infancy, childhood, teen years, adulthood, pregnancy/lactation, and aging.

It was my first test, and my highest score!

DOLLARS, DEBT, AND MYTHS

Chapter 7 Resource Summary:

United States Department of Education
www.ed.gov
College Affordability and Transparency
Center www.collegecost.ed.gov
Chronicle of Higher Education, news
www.chronicle.com
Tuition Exchange, employment in higher ed.
www.tuitionexchange.org

The Chronicle of Higher Education is a trade journal published for those of us working in higher education. Not a week goes by that budgets, dollars, debt, tuition, and return on investment are not discussed. These issues are headline news in the popular media, and the education industry is having a difficult time answering big questions.   I think most people, myself included, believe that a college education is an investment that is not strictly monetary. We don't *only* base our career on the highest pay, or *only* choose our college on the cheapest tuition. Not everything is black or white. There are shades of gray when making important decisions.

Keeping in mind the value of an educated mind, we can't forgo common sense and throw our children into debt that they'll carry into their marriage and potentially into bankruptcy. Graduating is not enough to justify the debt many will incur. Not all college graduates find work immediately, and many never find work in their field. Toss in increasing tuition costs, a little ignorance, and you've got a recipe for disaster.   The U.S. Department of Education maintains statistics on education, student loan debt, graduation rates, and just about anything related to education that you'd like to know. I'd like to open the chapter with some facts you can't ignore.

Student Loans

1.   A student loan is the only type of debt that cannot be discharged through bankruptcy.

2.   You must repay your loan even if you do not graduate.

3.   You must start repaying your loan 6 months from your last day of attendance, or from the date you drop below 6 credits.

4.   If you default on your payments, your income tax return and wages can be garnished.

5.   If you default on your payments, you will be banned from enlisting in the armed forces.

6.   If you default on your payments, your state held professional licenses will not be renewed (teacher, lawyer, nurse, nurse's aide, doctor, cosmetologist, accountant, etc.)

7.   Everyone who applies for a student will be given a student loan. (as long as they do not have a drug conviction or prior default)

8.   When loan money exceeds the cost of tuition, the student is

"refunded" the difference. This creates a system of students enrolling long enough to receive their "refund" check, and then withdrawing.

9.   Bachelor degree holders typically accumulate at least $25,000 in student loan debt before graduation.

Tuition

Since tuition isn't negotiable, are you just stuck paying it? No! You must remember there are hundreds, literally, hundreds of ways to get your child an accredited-respectable-legitimate degree without paying rack rate. I'm not going to send you on a wild-goose chase for obscure left-handed female bagpipe player scholarships. Most of those are a tremendous waste of time with only a tiny reward. In addition, any websites that claim to be scholarship clearinghouses are a SCAM and are to be avoided. Chasing scholarships is NOT the way to reduce your child's education cost.

I believe that the right price for a degree is one that meets the career needs of the student while not a burden financially. If your child is Harvard capable, you should try to get them into Harvard. The truth is, that less than 2 percent (that's 2 kids in 100) will have their application considered by an Ivy League college. Of those whose application is considered, 5% will be accepted! In other words, that's 1 child in 1000. This section is for the other 999.   The other 999 students need to go to school *somewhere*. Those students will join the ranks at any one of the other 2,700 accredited colleges in the United States. Many of which are interchangeably average. For a moment, I'd like you to forget everything you've ever considered about education. Even if you attended college, that was more than a few years ago, and things have changed! The options are fantastic, and the tuition is astonishing. As a homeschool parent, you are already primed to think outside the box. Doing so for your child's college tuition reaps HUGE benefits.

Free Tuition for Employees

This won't help all of you, but it could help many of you. Have you heard that college employee's children can attend college for free? Well, it's true. Within certain criteria, most colleges have provisions for the dependent children to attend the home college for reduced or no cost.

In the case of a community college, the benefit will be limited. Best case scenario, your child will earn 2 years of 100/200 level credit. Since community colleges are already a very affordable way to earn lower level credit, this "benefit" limits itself to a few thousand dollars per dependent. University employment is the golden goose. In nearly every university, dependent children can attend the home college for free. In programs like the Tuition Exchange (see opening list of resources) over 600 colleges participate in a reciprocal agreement that "exchanges" students for free or reduced tuition.

What kind of employment is eligible? Areas like: janitorial work, student services, foodservice, grounds or maintenance, tech support, bookstore, mailroom, resident life, etc. In other words, you don't have to be a professor to receive free tuition for your child(ren). In many, but not all, cases you must work full time, and possibly for a length of time prior to qualifying. In cases of part time work, wouldn't you mop floors a few nights a week in exchange for a pay check and a $150,000 degree? Once your child is in middle school, you should start scouting the local colleges and universities for employment opportunities.

It's also worth mentioning, that most schools have public databases of jobs, and many list job openings at www.higheredjobs.com. It's easy to scan the listings at your leisure. Full time Harvard employees can even enroll in degree programs for free! This might be an alternate entry option for a child literally wants to "work his way through college." The kids who apply traditionally will be paying full price. Be warned, however, it's expensive to live in Cambridge!

Community College Tuition

It's widely known that a community college is a less expensive option, but every year families still send their children off to four-year universities to take 100/200 level courses. Let's talk about community college tuition and the purpose of an AA/AS degree.

As you learned in an earlier chapter, not all associate degrees are created equal. In this instance, we'll discuss an AA degree (also AS degree) obtained for the sole purpose of transfer to a university. A community college is a 2-year college that meets the needs of the community. About half the students are pursuing a transfer degree (AA or AS) in general education (gen eds) and the other half are pursuing a trade or job training degree (AAS or AOS) which typically does not transfer anywhere.

A small, but growing segment of the community college population are non-enrolled students. They are not degree seekers, but they are attending noncredit courses that are directly related to job training. Sometimes these courses make up a certificate or diploma program. Courses in welding, nurse's aide, phlebotomy, computer skills, etc. are outside of the traditional enrollment tracks and are generally not covered by financial aid.
These courses are not for college credit and not part of a degree or transfer plan.

A transfer degree (AA or AS) typically consists of around 60 credits. These credits are "gen eds" and not part of a major. So, a student who wants to study business may have different gen eds than a student who wants to study biology, but in both cases they are not yet taking classes in their major. A community college charges by the credit, not the class. Current in-state rates in the United States are anywhere from $50 to $200, with the average landing around $100 per credit. If you're in a town with tuition on the high end, compare competing towns or even online. Most (98%) community colleges have classes online now, so you can even earn your AA in a different state. At the time of writing, the lowest online tuition in the United States at a community college is Clovis Community College in New Mexico.

Using simple math, you can see that $100 per credit x 60 credits places the cost of an AA or AS degree at around $6000. There are, of course, extraordinary fees for books (1-2 books per course, about $100 each) which can add no less than several thousand dollars. All total, your first 60 credits shouldn't cost more than $10,000. A real bargain, right? WRONG!

Remember CLEP? Taking 1-2 exams per year during high school yields no less than 1 year worth of credit! Simply planning 2 exams, especially high yield exams like College Math or French, take you into your community college career with between 30-45 credits. Deduct the savings of text books and add back the cost of testing. The results? An AA or AS degree for around $2,500-$3,500! Now THAT'S a bargain. If your family is on the lower end of the income range, your child will qualify for a Pell Grant (a gift) of $5,500 per year. The overpayment will be returned to your child. If you are following the math, you can pay as you go for CLEP exams in high school. When your child applies to community college, he qualifies for a $5,500 Pell Grant, about half of which will come back as a rebate in the form of cash.

State University Tuition

While we're discussing tuition, you should collect the costs of colleges you or your child may consider. With state university tuition hovering around $10,000 per year (plus housing, another $810,000) you can see why even the more affordable state university option is losing out to community college attendance. Without regard to cost, there are many people who feel strongly about attending a state university for the experience of it. Maybe it's the football, maybe it's the network, but they love their school. If this is the case, your child can attend the local community college under an ARTICULATION AGREEMENT. This is commonly called a transfer agreement. An articulation agreement is a signed document that states upon completion of the AA or AS degree from XYZ Community College, your child is guaranteed transfer as a junior into ABC University. There are many beautiful aspects to an articulation agreement which should be noted.

1.   You get the "brand" degree after attending only 2 years.

2.   An articulation means they'll accept all your credit, CLEP, AP, or other exams. Despite the university's own policy on CLEP, as long as you have completed your DEGREE per the agreement, you'll get a 100% transfer.

3.   You cut the cost of the degree in half by using exams, community college tuition, and staying home instead of using university housing the first 2 years.

4.   Cut the time to earn a degree from 4 years to 3 or less. CLEP during high school means starting community college as a junior.

5.   Immersion into the "college lifestyle" is gradual. Your child has 1+ year to acclimate to a heavier work-load, entering a formal class room, meeting new people, and eventually moving away from home.

The risk of this scenario is if you don't graduate from the community college with your transfer degree. Even one credit short voids your agreement. Yes, you still have your credit, but your transfer now involves individual evaluation of each credit/exam. In this case, and the case with all transfer credit, your old credit will be subject to new evaluation. You'll likely loose full semester's worth of credit (and tuition).

Private University Tuition

When you hear about astronomical student loan debt, you can bet they are talking about private tuition. Private universities, on average, cost $600 - $1200 per credit. Take a moment and read that again. Per credit.

Plus housing. Plus technology fees. Plus books. Plus parking. When your child graduates from a private undergraduate university, they are not a doctor, a lawyer, or a dentist. They hold a bachelor's. They enter the workforce with other bachelor's degree holders, and apply for grad school against other bachelor's degree holders. Statistically speaking, they'll enter an entry level job like every other bachelor's degree holder in the United States. Of course, they'll have more debt.

Tuition is now universally up over $100,000 and housing around $10,000 per year. The total tab to attend a private university will cost between $150,000 and $200,000! Unless you've saved that cash, that money will become debt your child must carry. Consider borrowing the equivalent of a mortgage with no money down at age 18. Except, a mortgage has better interest rates and allows for default.

Do I seem negative? Not at all. For many people, and in many industries, there are niche programs that really are the best of the best. Certain programs are a "golden tickets" into top careers. In this case, you're using the degree be among the most competitive in your field. For the majority, sadly, that isn't the case. Private universities are full of Liberal Arts majors, or other similarly undeclared majors. As I type this, headlines explode with the tales of debt and unemployment among college graduates.

Military Service

I'm a strong supporter of our military and all they do for our country. If you count your family among those who serve, I'd like to thank you for your service. Most people are aware that soldiers receive a "G.I. Bill" which essentially pays for their education after separation from the military. What many people don't know, however, is that all enlisted troops can take unlimited CLEP and DSST exams for free!

There are many motivated degree seekers who have located the most "CLEP/DSST friendly" accredited colleges in the country. As a result, many military can complete whole degrees through testing (for free). In that case, G.I. Bill money can be saved and used for an advanced degree later!

Delayed start & employer reimbursement

If your homeschooled child is enjoying exams, has completed or is close to completing his AA degree, he can continue testing while seeking full time employment. Thousands of employers offer employee reimbursement for tuition. This results in free or greatly reduced tuition.

While using the CLEP / AP exams to complete the general education requirements of the AA degree, your child can complete the grace period with their employer (generally 6-12 months). At that time, the employer will generally pay or reimburse the employee for a certain dollar amount of tuition. Sometimes there are additional requirements, so meet with human resources in advance.

One local company will pay for 12 credits (any dollar amount) per year for a degree associated with your job. A second will pay up to $5000 per year toward any degree. My husband's employer required 1 year of service in return for every year of college paid. In all cases, these are all valuable resources worth considering! In this case, the student used CLEP for the AA degree, and employer reimbursement to pay for the BA degree.

In-State vs. Out of State

It doesn't seem like a big deal, to attend college at a neighboring university, but check the prices. In an effort to serve the needs of their own state, many universities create such an inflated tuition rate that they hope to discourage out of state students. Out of state tuition is usually 2-3-4 times higher. Unless there is a specific specialty not offered in your home state, there probably isn't a compelling reason to pay out of state tuition.

An exception to the in-state vs. out of state tuition is often made for online programs. Many universities have an entire division devoted to online education. I'm not talking about "online colleges" rather your own state college that offers online options. These degrees, in almost every case, never say "online" on the degree. In addition, if the school is in your state, attending on campus or online won't be distinguished on a resume.   The intent is not to deceive, but to point out that there will often be different tuition prices for every school's online vs on-campus courses. Be sure to check both options.

Dual Enrollment

If you're lucky enough to live in a community that offers free dual-enrollment, you should utilize it to the fullest while your child is in high school. Most states, however, charge regular tuition to homeschooled students (despite offering free courses to public school enrolled students). It doesn't hurt to ask, however, for the same privileges as the public school students. Dual enrollment is a relatively new idea, and I'd estimate equal treatment isn't too far in the future. In the case of free dual enrollment, this is cheaper than a CLEP exam!

Free Colleges
From time to time, the news will report a college that is offering free tuition. Literally, zero dollars. Space doesn't allow us to review all of the potential schools and their requirements, but I've included a short list of totally free accredited degree-granting colleges for you can explore on our own!

- Cooper Union, New York City, NY
- Berea College, Berea, KY
- Deep Springs College, Big Pine, CA
- College of the Ozarks, Point Lookout, MO
- Military Academies (all)

Homemade Scholarships ($5,000 each)
As the homeschool parent, you have the ability to create one, or two, and maybe even three "homemade scholarships." I'm sure you're skeptical, but if you'll follow me through a simple scenario, I'll lay it out for you step by step.

This process yields one $5,000 homemade scholarship.

1. Commit to requiring 2 credit-earning courses per year of high school, and pass corresponding exams. (8 exams total)

2.   Commit to 2 years of solid foreign language study in addition to the 1 credit earning course. Pass your choice of foreign language exam from chapter 2)

3.   Commit to attending a college that accepts earned credit.

In the above recipe, the student will graduate high school with no less than 30 credits, but potentially more depending on the exams chosen. The acceptance of this credit from a college whose tuition is $165 per credit or more = $5,000!

In the above recipe, I hope you'll also see that passing 2 exams per school year is a very conservative program. These 2 exams can even be done in the summer, as to not interfere with your regular school schedule. I hope you also appreciate that this homemade scholarship has a shelf-life of 20 years. The same can't be said for any of the scholarships on the bulletin board at your local high school.

College Myths

Myth: Getting into college is the hardest part!
Truth: Getting into college is easy. Getting OUT of college, statistically speaking, is much harder. 25% will drop out in their first year, and of the remaining students, only 26% will ever graduate.
All will have paid tuition, and most leave with debt.

Myth: Going away to college is an important part of the educational experience.
Truth: The "socialization question" persists. Isn't this what they ask K-12 homeschools all the time? Going away to college as a freshman is the most expensive option, period. 56% of people who start college have dropped out or still not completed their degree after 6 years. The US Department of Education calls them "non-completers." For many, it was the "experience" that derailed their success. The next time someone shares their college "experience" you might ask them if that experience includes graduating.

Myth: My child isn't bright enough to attempt a CLEP, besides, if he fails, we are out $80.
Truth: Average people pass CLEP exams every day. Average people study, review suggested materials, take practice exams, and go in prepared. Reading ability aside, if your child is of average intelligence, he can

likely pass a CLEP. Besides, your child can fail the same exam <u>six times</u> before you've spent what it would cost at a community college once.

Myth: If my child doesn't get into X school, he won't have a promising future.
Truth: Even if your child does get into X school, there are no guarantees. The bottom line, your child should attend a regionally accredited college that awards degrees in his chosen field. In school he should work hard to pass his classes. In addition, networking, hard work and ambition are all better predictors of success.

Myth: Most people have a college degree, it's necessary for any job.
Truth: No, most people don't have a degree. In fact, only 27% of adults have an associate's or bachelor's degree. Fewer than 10% have a graduate degree (master's or PhD). It is true that most people attend college, but most people are not completers. For some career choices, a degree is required, but for many jobs a degree is optional or no help at all. In other cases, alternate criteria are required (job-specific certification). There are generally many options. Sometimes, delayed entry is a good plan. Using CLEP exams (good for 20 years), taking an apprenticeship, entering the work force, or serving in the military allow time to find the best path.

Myth: Since we homeschool, I'll just be happy if he gets into college, we'll worry about the cost later.

Truth: As you browse colleges, you'll notice most are well versed in homeschool admissions. It's not like it was 10 years ago. HSLDA has helped create a climate of fair and equal treatment. Many colleges even have dedicated advisors for homeschooled applicants. Do what is necessary in your state for your child to own a high school diploma (not GED) and apply with pride. Your child is not at a disadvantage; don't limit your choices to a few "homeschool friendly" (expensive) choices.

Lastly, compare CLEP/AP policy against other colleges. If your child is bringing in 30 credits, your child has a proven track record that they can do college level work. Any college would be lucky to have him enroll (and the tuition dollars he brings). In some cases, you can even fight to modify a poor or restrictive CLEP policy for those who follow in your child's footsteps. If a poor CLEP policy is stopping you from enrolling, tell them so.

Myth: Everyone has student loan debt.
Truth: Not everyone has student loan debt! Using credit earning options in high school is low-cost, and everyone can take advantage. Take your high school college credit to a CLEP-friendly community college for maximum transfer credit, and sign an articulation agreement into your state

university. If your child receives a Pell Grant for any/all of the 4 years of their education, and it isn't needed immediately for tuition, put it into a savings account for later. Attend college near your home or online to save on dorm costs. (Most state universities offer some of their degrees 100% online) 4 years of Pell Grant funds total up more than $20,000. Add in a part time job or scholarship and your child will graduate debt-free.

Myth: Borrowing $25,000 is no big deal; I'll easily make that in a year when I graduate. **Truth:** First off, there's interest and fees. Secondly, not everyone graduates. Fewer than half do, however, all debt must be repaid even if you don't graduate. Also, student loan payments are spread out over 10+ years, and as many as 26% will go into default. Finally, the employment rate among college graduates is at an all-time low. Even law school graduates are taking entry level positions previously filled by paralegals. It's a difficult economy to bank on a future salary that isn't a guarantee. With some planning and wise school choice, your child doesn't have to incur a large student loan debt.

It might also be an appropriate time to discuss how earning $30,000 does not mean you net $30,000. Your child, upon graduation, will be an adult with a lifestyle to match. Car, rent, food, laundry, utilities, etc. all reduce the "net" take home pay even

further. Most people struggle with the
discipline necessary to become debt-free.

Myth: My husband and I never went to
college; we'll need to rely on the experts to
help our child.
Truth: That was my myth. It's also the myth
I've heard other homeschool parents say too.
In short, ignorance is expensive! This book is
your springboard. Everything you need to
know is within your grasp. In a short time
you'll be planning like an expert, maybe even
helping other homeschool families too.
That's my truth.

TRANSCRIPTS

Chapter 8 Resource Summary:
- Home School Legal Defense Association www.hslda.org
- GPA Calculator www.back2college.com

Write a Transcript? No problem!

Creating a transcript can be intimidating. Yes, you need to create a transcript for your child's high school career. No, you don't need to start in kindergarten. Yes, it should be complete with grades and GPA. No, you don't need to create a portfolio. Yes, one page is enough. Now that all of that is out of the way, let's look at what you need to do (don't need to do) and how credit earning courses will be presented on your transcript.

A good friend of mine is an administrator at a small, private (expensive) Christian university. He told me he'd just finished reviewing the application of a homeschooled applicant and decided not to admit the student. I asked why, and he went on to explain that the student's reading list really included too many books that (he felt) were not rigorous high school reading. I asked how in the world he knew what books this child read? His reply "it was on his transcript."

Zonk!

A transcript is not a portfolio. It's not a place for reading lists, projects, names of text books, or brands of curriculum. A transcript is a list of course titles your child has completed. Following each course title is a grade, and the quantity of credit awarded. In addition to some other general information like: name, address, birth date, graduation date, and maybe an extracurricular activity, nothing else belongs on a transcript!

Here is a simple transcript for 1 semester:

Grade 9
Fall (08/01/11 – 12/18/11)

Algebra 1 (.5 cr) A
9th Grade English (.5 cr) A
College Prep U.S. History 1 (.5 cr) A
Guitar (.5 cr) A
9th Grade Science (.5 cr) B

Notice the simple titles. The curriculum brands are not part of the titles. In fact, you may use multiple brands to create what becomes "9th grade English." Perhaps your English course consists of IEW writing, a classical literature reading list, an REA guide, and grammar workbook. Despite the fact that YOU approach these as separate subjects, they are in fact still "9th Grade English" and would be listed as such. Keep it simple, keep it clear.

Grade 9
Fall (08/01/11 – 12/18/11)

Algebra 1 (.5 cr) A
9th Grade English (.5 cr) A
College Prep U.S. History 1 (.5 cr) A
Guitar (.5 cr) A
9th Grade Science (.5 cr) B

Also, notice the use of "College Prep" in the history course. In this instance, the family used the CLEP U.S. History 1 exam to award the student college credit. Whether or not college credit was earned isn't completely relevant to his high school transcript. Later, if the student takes a *college class,* online or at the local community college, then you'll certainly identify the class as Dual Enrollment.

Speak "college" not "homeschool" language

The mistake parents make, is they tend to over validate. By that I mean that they go to great efforts to validate their homeschool. To prove that their child did something! In this effort, you'll see over-sharing. Like the mom who sent her entire child's reading list, or the family that lists every curriculum ever used, this is too much information. Colleges are not qualified to evaluate high school curriculum, and colleges don't know brands. Your local public school isn't sending curriculum information on their students, and neither should you.

Colleges are used to a very plain and very simple transcript system. They get hundreds, sometimes thousands of plain and simple transcripts every year. If your transcript is unusual, it likely won't impress them, instead, it will likely confuse them.

While you and I know that Saxon is a well-respected math curriculum, I'll mail you ten cents if you can find an advisor who knows what Saxon math is. Advisors don't know what "Saxon" is, so they can't evaluate it. "Saxon" isn't a subject. Advisors **do** know what "Algebra" is or what "French" is. You must speak to them in their language if you want them to evaluate your child's transcript properly.

As you choose courses and curriculum for your child, consider the title you will use to identify the course. For instance, "foundations" or "essentials" may be part of how you choose a level for your classroom; but it's not the title of a course. To a college, "Foundations of English" translates into remedial English. Keep things simple. 9th Grade English is an excellent title.

Additionally, in courses where you meld history and English, or Latin and logic, consider listing them as separate courses with one title "A.P. Western Civilization" and then awarding appropriate extra credit. Alternatively, you may consider dividing them into separate courses with individual titles, and again, using appropriate (partial) credit that reflects the contact hours. Use the method that best describes what happened in your homeschool classroom.

My child did this really cool thing...

Your child's essay, if required by admission committee, is where they explain their interesting lifestyle or unique learning opportunities. If an essay isn't required, or if the college is open enrollment (all qualified applicants are admitted, like at a community college) then that information may not appear anywhere on their admission application. It's simply not required.

Elaborating dilutes efficacy

I've noticed a trend among homeschool advice books and articles to elaborate a transcript, but my advice is the polar opposite. Your transcript should be vanilla in style, closely resembling that of their peers. If you'd like to see a real high school transcript, contact your old high school and request yours. This will help keep you on point.   In your effort to elaborate and demonstrate what a well-rounded and enriching curriculum you provided (its ok, homeschooling was hard work and we're proud!) you can sometimes shoot yourself in the foot.

In this example, this family put great attention into the humanities, providing a thorough and comprehensive approach to teaching the English language. (We will leave off their other courses to keep focus)

9th Grade
Writing: Poetry
American Literature

10th Grade
Writing: Prose
Classic English Literature

11th Grade
African Literature
Public Speaking

While the parent is attempting to demonstrate an exceptional understanding and application of Language Arts, a traditional college may classify these courses as "electives" not "English." English is English. Literature (in college-speak) is a class that is not English. Writing, (in college-speak) is remedial English. Again, the composition of your courses is your own. The titles, however, should be very simple.

If a college asks for more information, and you wish to provide it, you can prepare a simple outline of the topics or theme of your courses. Like this:

9th Grade English
Narrative writing, report writing, persuasive writing, grammar, poetry, reading comprehension, reading analysis, significant works of selected American authors.

Optionally, you may also want to include enrichment activities that were part of the course. Examples of enrichment activities include small articles or stories reprinted in a club or church newsletter, an editorial submission to the newspaper, or a self-published poetry collection. These are examples of how an exceptional student applied their learning in a unique way. Of course, for the majority of us, simply a title will suffice.

Biographical Information
The transcript must include complete biographical information. While I suggest

your transcript be only 1 page long, if it is longer, the biographical information should be at the top of every page.

Name, address, birth date, social security number, and phone number are standard. Feel free to leave off the social security number, but it will likely be requested prior to enrollment.

Grades

Colleges evaluate incoming freshman (sometimes) through their GPA. This stands for "Grade Point Average." The GPA is a numerical calculation that is weighted against the level of difficulty. In short, an "A" in a general class is *worth less* than an "A" in a college level class. Many families (including mine) don't issue grade, report cards, or calculate GPA as part of our school routine. In fact, in our house, every course is completed until it is mastered, not according to the speed that it is mastered; so all courses are "A" grades.

I appreciate that a college admissions representative may assume a parent has "grade bias" against their child, so I always temper my requirement for competency against their overall understanding or mastery. In other words, I give a grade on a transcript; I don't give grades in our day-to-day.

For example, in a homeschool that requires every math problem to be completed from every math lesson, it's not likely that the student earned 100% on every lesson. However, it is likely that you had your student go back and re-work all missed questions. This is what is referred to as 100% competency. So, while this is the standard in our home, this is not to suggest that all of the children meet that standard equally. For some children, their understanding is slower or less

To bridge the gap between what we do and how we report that on paper, you have to create a meter your child can be measured against. Staying roughly inside of those expectations will make grade calculation pretty simple.

Here are some tips:

- If you're going to use letter grades, use A, B, C, D, F not a home-made letter system. If you use your own letter system at home, roughly convert them into a standard A-F scale.

- Minus and plus grades are fine, but they make calculating GPA twice as difficult. It's a personal decision.

- If you absolutely refuse to issue a grade, from which a GPA can be calculated, simply provide a pass/fail system on the transcript.

Stick to one method

Pick one system and stay with it all 4 years. If you start using grades, but decide later to go to a "pass/fail" system, then go back and simply record all passing grades (A, B, C) as "pass" rather than having a mixed system on the transcript. Additionally, if you start out using pass/fail and switch to grades, try your best to convert the earlier grades into letter grades for ease of understanding and consistency. An excellent online GPA calculator can be found in the tools tab at www.Back2college.com.

Keeping up to date

The beginning or end of each semester is an excellent time to visit your child's transcript. If you save the file on your computer, you'll have a simple file that can be opened and updated whenever necessary. At the start and close of each year, ask yourself these key questions:

Q: What is the name of the course planned/completed?
A: It's possible that the focus initially planned has changed, or that new material has redirected learning goals and a new course name may be more appropriate. For instance, if you initially started "General Biology with Lab" course but ultimately spent the entire term studying only human biology, it's appropriate to title the transcript as Human Biology; Additionally, if you intended on completing a lab

component, but didn't, you'll want to remove the words "with lab" from the title.

Q: *How many credits are planned/completed?*
A: Typically, the number of contact hours would determine the number of credits issued. Schools have a very specific method of calculation that determines credit hours. The Carnegie unit is one type, contact hours, or other methods can be used. In a homeschool setting, hours spent in a subject may be less than in a traditional school setting.

A typical course of 9th grade English may require about an hour per day. Assuming your school runs Monday-Friday, a full semester (1/2 year) will equate to ½ credits. During this time, the student would complete roughly half of the curriculum. During the second half of the school year, the student on the same schedule would complete roughly the remaining half for another ½ credits. The full year of 9th grade English would be worth 1 full credit. If this roughly represents your situation, then rounding up or down is harmless. Running a few weeks short of finishing, or finishing a few weeks early are not significant, simply round the hours.

To give a second example, if your child enrolls in a local driver's education course, that course would likely NOT be considered a full semester (1/2 credit) and in that example, a ¼ credit could be awarded, with a different subject filling the remaining ¼ credit slot that term.

Q: *What grade did my child earn?*
A: That isn't as straight-forward a question as you may think. Unless you're using curriculum that assesses the student, you may never go through the trouble of calculating grades on anything other than tests or quizzes. Keep in mind that a formal school setting uses grades as a method of evaluating large groups of progress frequently, and logging it for a number of reasons. A homeschool family rarely operates this way. As a parent, you may have a good sense of your child's true understanding of a subject. For instance, your child may complete the assignments, but despite doing so correctly, doesn't really understand the material. I've found this in my own homeschool, especially when we use workbooks or other short answer worksheets.

With the significance of GPA, a parent may really struggle with the assignment of a grade. Some parents feel guilty awarding an "A" for fear that it "looks" bias in favor of their child. I would encourage you to step away from the peer pressure, and use your best judgment. One bad unit or one poor paper does not mean your child must suffer a poor grade. On the other hand, grade inflation isn't the answer. Did your child complete the assignments? Were they done well, or very well? Do they have a good understanding of the theme of the course? Can they have a verbal discussion about aspects of the course? Can they dictate back what they have learned? My favorite measure is if the course changed their intuition about the subject.

A less common, though completely acceptable alternative is to simply grade the course "pass/fail" without assigning a letter grade. If you adopt this method, do so consistently for the entire year. No GPA is calculated in this case.

Q: *Did my child earn college credit?*
A: If you are structuring your curriculum around credit-earning options, you'll likely have multiple courses that match up with CLEP/AP/DSST exams. One thing to remember is that even if your child did not *pass* an exam, they still completed the course, and they should receive full course credit. Suppose your child spent a semester studying biology with the intent of taking the biology CLEP exam. After a semester of study, they attempted the exam, but did not pass. This is not a failure! They still studied biology for a semester, and should be awarded the full credit (1/2 credit) accordingly. Perhaps a second semester will result in a re-take, or perhaps they'd like to move on to something else, but don't let the CLEP exam dictate the credit/grade for your child's high school course. Public schools that offer AP courses do not rely on the student's AP exam score at all, in fact, it has

no bearing on the class and it shouldn't in your school either.

If your child does pass an exam, you'll have to pick a method for recording that credit. There are two schools of thought on how to accomplish this. First, you could simply do nothing. Record the transcript as a course in biology, and later, when your child applies to college they will submit both transcripts (high school and CLEP) at which time the college will determine the college credit awarded. The second school of thought is to incorporate the additional "weight" of college credit into the transcript. So, in a typical 1 semester biology course, a student may earn ½ credit; but a student that passed a CLEP exam may earn 1 full credit that semester. An asterisk * or other marking can indicate on the transcript that this course yielded college credit. You can use the same technique for AP or DSST.

In my opinion, the better method is the first method, where the college credit is completely separate from the high school credit. You should know that this is an issue I've argued with a few fellow parents about. You should know that neither options are "right" or "wrong" rather just a different choice. There are good arguments for weighting a grade when a student is applying to a competitive college, so in that instance I would be in favor of weighted courses.

I believe that keeping the high school curriculum simple is the best method because you don't have to explain or justify a non-traditional credit system or grades. You don't have to provide a "key" for the reader to translate your process, and sometimes the CLEP may not match perfectly with the title of the high school course, which I think may cause confusion. I like a simple ½ credit per course per semester approach, and this is consistent with my suggestion that admissions representatives are not adept at evaluating nontraditional transcripts.

Lastly, with the increasing popularity of dual enrollment, I've noticed a few colleges making changes to their policies. In more than one instance, I've noticed statements indicating that courses completed as part of a high school transcript are not eligible for use as college credit toward a degree, but instead only used for advanced standing (sometimes called double dipping). At the risk of CLEP/AP/DSST falling into this category, I like to keep it off the transcript. To emphasize, this does not mean your child gets less credit, it is exactly the same credit presented on two documents instead of one. When in doubt, leave it out.

Q: Did my child participate in organized sports, clubs, or other noteworthy activities?
A: Traditional high school transcripts list participation in sports or school newspaper simply at the bottom. You can do this for your child too.
Here is a simple way to recognize those activities:

Church choir: 9, 10, 11
Junior Achievement: 9, 10
Boy Scouts: 9, 10, 11, 12
Homeschool Basketball Team: 11, 12

Finally, there are dozens of websites that guide you through the transcript writing process. You can, in fact, even hire consultants to write a transcript for you. I hope you'll find such services unnecessary, and take pride in building your child's record of academic accomplishments.

TAKING YOUR CREDIT TO COLLEGE

Chapter 9 Resource Summary:

* United States Department of Education Accreditation Database Search Engine www.ope.ed.gov/accreditation
* Home School Legal Defense Association www.hslda.org
* Bear's Guide to Distance Learning, Dr. John Bear

This chapter looks at college choice considerations as they relate to the credit your child earned over the past 4 years in homeschool. Often, someone asks "Can my child take his CLEP credit to Yale?" The answer is "no" but I often want to ask if their child has been accepted to Yale? There are over 2,700 accredited 4 year colleges in the United States, and only 8 schools make up the Ivy League. This chapter is for the 99.98% of college applicants, some of whom may get accepted to Yale, but mostly for everyone else.

Look at data from the 2011 Census. Our educational attainment is at an all-time high.

99% 8th grade completion
85% High school graduate
57% some college, not graduated
40% associate degree
26% bachelor's degree
8% master's degree
3% doctorate or professional degree.

If only 40% of the population hold an associate or bachelor degree, what about the other 60%? More than half of those who start college will never finish, yet they take their student loans with them into their life. *Completing any type of college degree is something that only 40% of Americans have done!* It's an accomplishment!

The majority of Americans do not hold a college degree, though it doesn't seem that way if you follow the media. The "non-degree holders" may have entered the workforce, started their own business, completed an apprenticeship, or entered the armed forces. Their job prospects vary wildly, but they do represent the majority of Americans. This chapter isn't intended to replace thorough planning and college selection. There are, literally, thousands of books that tear apart the details of each American college. This book also isn't going to battle out college rankings, fuss about endowments, research grants, big 10 football, or party atmosphere. Frankly, I'm of the opinion that the best college degree is the one that is completed. College isn't for everyone, but if it's the path for your child, make sure they finish! I often hear parents say they want their child to GET INTO COLLEGE. As you know by now, I'd like my kids to GET OUT of college. Preferably with a degree. 57% of students enroll, and leave college without their degree. In addition to the financial burden this creates on a young person, it also creeps back up time and time again as they apply for jobs. Is it ethical to list an "almost" degree on a resume? No. A degree is either completed, or not completed. Misrepresenting yourself can be grounds for termination. As colleagues climb the ranks, often adults become frustrated that they didn't complete their degree, and may return to college time and time again to do so. This isn't an exception, it's the rule. The majority of people will spend their lives in on-again, off-again credit seeking. Most will never have anything to show for it.

Having the right mindset is essential when you help your child pick a college. Understanding the 3 big barriers will help you set him up for success. Face these "degree killers" now, plan for them, and plan a work-around.

Time

Time is the number one degree killer. Most students languish for 2, 4, or 6+ years working on their first degree until they drop out. Why? Start with a few remedial courses, add in a few prerequisites, and take less than 12 credits per semester; you've just added 2 more years to your 4 year degree! Factor in earning a living, car payments, marriage, and children, and you've got the typical frustrated twenty-something college student. Most people don't have the stamina or endurance to complete an entire degree as a full time student, and even if they do, the cost of attending college for additional years is daunting. As life is happening, frustrations set in and the student slows down or drops out.

You already know how to beat Killer Time! Since testing in high school allows your child to shave time off the front end of their degree immediately, you must choose a college that will reward your child's hard work. Previous chapters show you how to earn 15, 30, 60, or more credit in high school. Walking in with ¼ or ½ of a degree complete increases the likelihood that your child will finish. Choose a college with generous CLEP/AP/DSST policy. Even without 100% transfer, reducing any time required will be beneficial.

Money

When you appreciate that an $80 CLEP exam yields the same credit as a $700 community college course, or as a $2,000 private college course, it changes how you look at college costs.   It is unnecessary to graduate from college with tens of thousands in student loan debt. Maxing out on your college's CLEP/AP/DSST testing allowance cuts college costs dramatically. One caution: before finalizing your decision, compare the college's CLEP/AP/DSST policy against the cost of the remaining credit. A college that accepts all of your child's credit isn't as affordable if the remaining credits cost $100,000! You want to find a balance between a generous credit policy and affordable tuition.

An additional aspect of cost is the expense of dorm living. Any college credit earned in high school will shave significant time off the degree, which in turn shaves of time spent in a dorm. In many cases, this can save more than $10,000 per year!

Socialization

Isn't it ironic that in the years of homeschooling, you've had to answer the question "what about socialization?" yet socialization is precisely the reason many students drop out /flunk out of college; too much socialization! Testing allows your child to bypass much of the "freshman experience" and in some cases, earn the entire bachelor's degree from home. If or when your child enters college, or even graduate school, many of the freshmen have "socialized" their way right out of college and cleared the way for the serious student.

What are the good colleges?

There are currently more than 4,080 accredited two and four year colleges in the United States. For over 5 years, I've poured over thousands of catalogs and website, forum archives, and books. I've tirelessly evaluated policy, compared time/cost ratios, and reviewed CLEP/AP/DSST acceptance guidelines. In short, there are **hundreds of excellent** options for your consideration. Of course, you may have criteria that are important to your family (close to home, specific major, student teacher ratio, religious preference, scholarship or sports opportunities, etc.). For my book, I left those criteria out. Specific criteria are just that, specific. I used very different criteria to best meet the needs of who might be reading my book.

Criteria for my <u>good colleges</u>
list:
- Regionally Accredited
- Exam credit friendly CLEP/AP/DSST
- Credit-transfer (because you can price shop)
- Distance learning or non-traditional options
- Homeschool friendly (admissions criteria)
- Cost (well-planned vs rack rate)
- Must offer a 4-year degree (bachelor)

I've narrowed my list to 10. Not "top 10" but simply 10. I like, and will work for most of my readers. I'm sure there are others, and perhaps I'll revise my list in a future edition. For now, I'm comfortable suggesting that any of the 10 on this list will blend perfectly into a Homeschooling for College Credit plan.

All 10 of the colleges are regionally accredited.
This means they hold the gold standard accreditation, are "legitimate" schools (not "degree mills") and credit earned is likely to transfer to other regionally accredited colleges. They are all recognized by the United States Department of Education, and all participate in traditional financial aid programs.

All 10 are **highly likely** to award exam credit (CLEP, DSST, AP) and accept transfer credit from your local community college.

Should I choose a college or a university?

In the United States, there is no appreciable difference. There are some nuances which you may find helpful as you start to read about colleges and universities, especially if you're researching higher education for the first time.

Many universities are made up of colleges within the university (College of Nursing, College of Liberal Arts, College of Education, etc.). Frequently a university offers online or distance versions of their degrees through a specific "college" at the university. For instance, the college of Continuing Education at Harvard University offers associate, bachelor, and master's degrees. These degrees are 100% Harvard University degrees, but few people know about them because they are tucked away in the Continuing Education College.

Some colleges still have colleges within them. My degree at Thomas Edison State College was earned through the Heavin College of Arts and Sciences. Most colleges and universities have divisions, or colleges, that teach various majors.
It's all under the same umbrella.

You'll notice some of the colleges on my list have a specific campus or designation. Be sure to follow the correct address to the correct college. Some universities have up to 10 or more colleges within their system, all offering degrees, and you'll soon find that they are all priced differently! The college or campus listed here is already the best price option.

I've included two types of cost, the "well planned degree" cost which assumes you've followed my suggestions for maximum testing, community college transfer when possible, living at home or taking courses via distance learning, and maintaining full time student status.

The "rack rate" degree price assumes you're just walking in and signing up. I'll assume that no remedial work is required, no testing credits are brought in, no transfer credits are brought in, and that your child will complete all 120 credits at that campus in 4 years. (Dorm not included)

No one college has the "best" in every category, but this list represents a good balance. Notice, even the schools on this list can get very expensive if you're not using good planning strategy! All of the schools on this list are homeschool friendly. A homeschool friendly college is one that requires little to no additional requirements above that of a traditionally-schooled applicant. At one time, college admission personnel placed homeschool graduates in the same category of "drop-outs" but that is changing! Many colleges even have a dedicated staff member or department that specializes in ushering your homeschool graduate through the admission process. If you are asking for an exception, for instance to allow your high school student to enroll prior to graduation, that may require more effort. Four of the colleges (Charter Oak, Excelsior, Harvard, and Thomas Edison State) frequently allow high school students to dual-enroll, but a simple request must be made ahead of registering. Harvard encourages high school students to pursue their AA in place of a homeschool diploma, which then transfers perfectly into a bachelor's degree program. There are options, good ones!

If, at any time, you encounter hostile admissions personnel, a phone call to HSLDA is suggested. HSLDA have successfully fought for the fairness on behalf of homeschool graduates, and continue to do so when it's brought to their attention. This not only helps your family, but other homeschool graduates too!

10 Good Colleges (Alphabetical)

Charter Oak State College
55 South Perimeter Road, New Britain, CT 06053
(860) 515-3800
www.charteroak.edu
Generous CLEP/AP/DSST policy
Accepts 100% transfer credit
1 Cornerstone course, 1 Capstone course required
On-line only
Homeschool students write a letter asking for age waiver $322/credit
Well-planned degree will cost $3,000 - $9,000
Rack rate degree will cost $30,000 - $39,000

Colorado State University – Global Campus
8000 E. Maplewood Ave., Bldg. 5, Suite 250
Greenwood Village, CO 80111
1-800-920-6723
www.CSUglobal.edu
Generous CLEP/AP/DSST policy
Accepts 90 credits in transfer
Straighterline partner school. On-line only
Homeschool students can apply during high school if they have 13 credits (CLEP/AP/DSST/Straighterline)
$350/credit
Well-planned degree will cost $12,500 - $15,500
Rack rate degree will cost $42,000

Excelsior College
7 Columbia Circle, Albany, NY 12203 1-855-323-9235 www.excelsior.edu
Generous CLEP/AP/DSST/ACE policy – no cap
Accepts all transfer credit. On-line only
No add'l admission requirements for home school students
$ 390/credit plus enrollment fee
Well-planned degree will cost $9,000 - $11,000
Rack rate degree will cost $47,000 - $50,000

Harvard University – Continuing Education
(also called "Harvard Extension")
51 Brattle Street, Cambridge, MA 02138
1-617-495-4024
www.harvard.edu
Accepts 12 CLEP/AP credit
Accepts 64/128 transfer credits
Hybrid on-line and on campus degree
Associate, bachelors, masters degrees available. Homeschool students encouraged to attend during high school and complete their AA. No additional requirements for admission
$261/credit ($1045/course)
Well-planned degree will cost $17,000 - $22,000
Rack rate degree will cost $33,440

Illinois State University
201 Hovey Hall, Normal, Illinois 61790
1-800-366-2478
www.illinoisstate.edu
CLEP policy: not generous, however, any AA
or AS degree from any regionally accredited
college in the United States awards a full
transfer of 60 credits. The transfer overrides
the university's CLEP policy.
Accepts any AA / AS degree for transfer
On-line and on-campus options
No add'l admission requirements for home
school students
$410/credit IN STATE, $578/credit OUT-OF-
STATE
Well-planned degree will cost $28,000-
$34,000
Rack-rate degree will cost $50,000 - $70,000

Penn State University - World Campus
128 Outreach Building, University Park, PA
16802
1-800-252-3592
www.worldcampus.psu.edu
Generous CLEP/AP/DSST policy
Transfer credit up to half of degree (60/120)
On-line only (campus based differs in
policy/cost)
$504/credit
Well-planned degree will cost $31,000 -
$39,000
Rack rate degree will cost $61,000

Southern New Hampshire University
2500 North River Road, Manchester, NH,
03106
800-668-1249
www.snhu.edu
Generous CLEP/AP/DSST policy
Accepts 90 credits in transfer
On-line and on-campus options
Homeschool supplement form required for
admission
$320/credit (on-line tuition rate)
Well-planned degree will cost $9,600-$15,000
Rack-rate degree ON-LINE PROGRAM $39,000
Rack-rate degree CAMPUS PROGRAM
$110,000 - $130,000

Thomas Edison State College
101 W. State Street, Trenton, NJ 08608
1-888-442-8372
www.tesc.edu
Generous CLEP/AP/DSST policy – no cap,
accepts
ACE credit
Accepts 100% transfer credit
1 Capstone course required
On-line only
Homeschool students write a letter asking
for age waiver
$ 165-221/credit plus enrollment fee
Well-planned degree will cost $2,500 - $7,500
Rack rate degree will cost $20,000 - $36,000

University of Wyoming - Outreach
1000 E. University Ave. Laramie, WY 82071
1-307-766-1121
www.uwyo.edu
Generous CLEP/AP/DSST policy – no cap
Accepts 90 credits in transfer
On-line and on-campus options
No add'l admission requirements for homeschool students
$106/credit (on-line tuition rate)
Well-planned degree will cost $6,500 - $9,500
Rack rate degree ON-LINE PROGRAM will cost $13,000
Rack rate degree CAMPUS PROGRAM $108,000 - $112,000

Upper Iowa University
605 Washington Street, Fayette, IA 52142
1-800-553-4150
www.uiu.edu
Generous CLEP/AP/DSST policy
Accepts 78-90 transfer credits
On-line and on-campus options available No add'l admission requirements for homeschool students
$348/credit online, $296 independent study
Well-planned degree will cost $14,000 to $18,000
Rack rate degree will cost $42,000

Distance Learning

Distance learning as a category is beyond the scope of this book. However, the best college-by-college resource for strictly *distance learning* schools is The Bears' Guide to Distance Learning by John Bear PhD.

In closing, I hope you've found numerous ways to boost your curriculum, add layers of enriching experiences, earn college credit, and save a bunch of money. Finally, what is true today can (and will) change at some point. Until your child is enrolled, they are not "locked" into any policy; so while planning now, please remember to be flexible and adaptable. There is no perfect path, no perfect curriculum, and no perfect way. (If there were, EVERYONE would be doing it!)

My wish is that you'll enjoy the remainder of your homeschool journey through until the very end.

Follow Homeschooling for College Credit daily on Facebook!

INDEX